I0134999

SELF ESTEEM

Boost Your Confidence and Improve Your Self-esteem

(The Beginners Guide to Build and Increase Your Confidence and Improve Your Social Skills)

Melissa Hatton

Published by Jackson Denver

Melissa Hatton

All Rights Reserved

Self Esteem: Boost Your Confidence and Improve Your Self-esteem (The Beginners Guide to Build and Increase Your Confidence and Improve Your Social Skills)

ISBN 978-1-77485-253-8

All rights reserved. No part of this guide may be reproduced in any form without permission in writing from the publisher except in the case of brief quotations embodied in critical articles or reviews.

Legal & Disclaimer

The information contained in this book is not designed to replace or take the place of any form of medicine or professional medical advice. The information in this book has been provided for educational and entertainment purposes only.

The information contained in this book has been compiled from sources deemed reliable, and it is accurate to the best of the Author's knowledge; however, the Author cannot guarantee its accuracy and validity and cannot be held liable for any errors or omissions. Changes are periodically made to this book. You must consult your doctor or get professional medical advice before using any of the suggested remedies, techniques, or information in this book.

Upon using the information contained in this book, you agree to hold harmless the Author from and against any damages, costs, and expenses, including any legal fees potentially resulting from the application of any of the information provided by this guide. This disclaimer applies to any damages or injury caused by the use and application, whether directly or indirectly, of any advice or information presented, whether for breach of contract, tort, negligence, personal injury, criminal intent, or under any other cause of action.

You agree to accept all risks of using the information presented inside this book. You need to consult a professional medical practitioner in order to ensure you are both able and healthy enough to participate in this program.

TABLE OF CONTENTS

Introduction

Self-esteem is a unique kind of energy that is buried in each of us. It encompasses the natural sense of self-worth that is probably our personal claim to fame -- that sparkling glow that we, who are instructors or psychotherapists try to create in those who are working with us. This sparkle is the way to build self-esteem.

While you are reading this book, it's important to understand what I mean when I say "self-esteem." There are a myriad of definitions that I consider to be misleading and less motivating or less effective than the one I have presented. When self-esteem ceases to have its true significance and falls to a modest expression, it could not be observed by those who strive to attain them -- the very people who need it most. There's nothing more satisfying than being able to prove how precious remarkable, admirable, and important you are. It is your opportunity to feel confident in yourself.

Self-esteem could be the answer to modern-day life. It is viewed as the key to financial success, wellbeing, and satisfaction for individuals, and is considered to be the answer to wrongdoing, failure and abuse of drugs. Self-esteem is also widely recognized in scholastic circles. As with the study of character and mentality research, it has an important role in the models that involve influence, compliance, emotional conflicts as well as physical and emotional wellbeing as well as social examinations just to mention a few examples.

The extensive fascination of self-esteem is a proof of its importance but it also leads to unintended consequences. Self-esteem is being portrayed small, it is difficult to comprehend its real meaning. Researchers study how high or low self-esteem affects people according to their thoughts and feelings. In the end, there is a variance an assortment of analysts conduct research on the impact of different experiences on the way individuals perceive themselves) and also an interfering variables (with the requirement that a individuals with high self-esteem to be able to activate a wide range of mental strategies).

Self-esteem has become an evolving concept, with structure constantly altering the value of it is at risk of being eroded.

In this issue this issue, we examine fundamental characteristics, starting areas, and components of self-esteem. In this instance I'll pose the following question what do we mean when we say "self-esteem and what are the characteristics be associated with self-esteem that is high versus low? I will look at the initial stages in self-esteem. The question here is the kinds of experiences that lead to self-esteem that is high and what contributes will lead to negative self-esteem. The notion of self-esteem being a significant factor will be examined along with other different views on the issue.

The main issue that will guide this book will be the traits of self-esteem in itself. Some therapists use an instinctual approach to grasp any kind of self-esteem. The theory asserts that self-esteem is an expression of pride in one's own identity which is developed primarily through instinctive or unreasonable methods (unreasonable in this case means "not based on rationale"). Different doctors take an cognitive approach. They recognize that self-esteem is an opinion that people form about themselves. The ability to discern is, in large part dependent on how one appraises of one's capabilities and qualities.

The previous method examines self-esteem in relation to feelings of affection, which generally are not a good idea or even smart The last method compares self-esteem to the choices individuals make regarding their worth and value as individuals.

Self-esteem can not be the type that comes from a gift (at times, it could be) that you're brought to the world. It comes from consistent repetition and small successes which eventually lead to huge triumphs. You can build confidence in yourself and, as you keep up positive habits your self-esteem will continue growing.

A lot of people are embarrassed by themselves at least once in a while. Self-esteem issues could be triggered by having been treated in a negative way by someone else recently or before, or the individual's own view of themselves. This is common. But, low self-esteem can be common among the majority of people especially those who suffer from fear, anxiety, sadness and hallucinations or suffer from disability or illness. If you're one of the above, you could feel depressed about yourself in a way that is unnecessary. Self-esteem issues prevent you from enjoying the world around you, doing the things you have to accomplish, and advancing toward your personal goals.

You are entitled to be a lover of yourself. However, it can be difficult to feel proud of yourself when you're under constant worry about having adverse effects that are difficult to control when suffering from disabilities, encounter difficulties or when people are treating your needs with a harsh attitude. In these cases it's difficult to avoid being drawn into an downward spiral of low self-esteem and less self-esteem.

For instance, you might begin to feel bad at yourself when someone speaks to your character, you're facing numerous constraints at work, or you're struggling to coexist with a family member. Then , you begin giving yourself negative self-talk like "I'm useless." This could lead to you developing negative thoughts about yourself and your own self that could lead you to think of doing something that hurts you or someone else like drinking excessive amounts of alcohol, or screaming at your kids. Through the use of the concepts and exercises found in this book, you will be able to refrain from doing things that make you feel down and make choices that inspire you to be more positive about yourself.

This piece will offer suggestions on how you can do to improve yourself in order to boost self-esteem. These ideas are derived from people like you who recognize that they are self-conscious and want to increase it.

If you try the techniques in this book, and other methods you could consider to boost your confidence, you might notice you are experiencing feelings of insecurity from positive feelings about yourself. This is common. Don't give these feelings the chance to stop you from being happy with yourself. They will diminish, since you feel better and happier about yourself. To alleviate the pain allow your friends to understand the emotions you're feeling. Take a good break whenever you are able to. Do things to relax such as thinking about the cleaning process.

One of the most important points this book makes is that confidence isn't an effortless, jovial wonder. The need for it is embedded in our nature and, if we comprehend the need, we realize that it is not attainable with self-confidence or in the midst of any kind of interest that happens to attract us. Self-esteem is based on the proper exercise of the brain and what that means is explored in the chapters later. We will discover that self-esteem and discernment, perseverance, self-dedication and personal uprightness are inextricably linked.

It is also important to note that, despite the fact that others might encourage us or hinder us in our quest for self-esteem, particularly when we are young, no one can give us self-esteem. It has to come from within.

Chapter 1: Confidence for children in childhood

I vividly remember asking my mom how small children could tell that other children looked attractive. My mother told me that children transmit how others treat the most beautiful children. While physical beauty can attract more interest and, in certain instances, even special favors but confidence can bring you more.

Watch the children, and you'll notice the people who lead the group as well as the ones who follow. There are others who are lonely or are strangers. When you witness a bunch of children in the park, you'll be able to identify all the different kinds of people.

The children who are leaders tend to be the most secure. The ones who follow them generally are confident however not nearly as much as their leader.

Children who are less well-known are not confident or have no confidence. This is the case for those who are victims of harassing or any other undesirable behavior that children aren't the only ones to exhibit.

What is the reason that some children are safe and others not? This question is often discussed during therapy sessions for children who turn into adults.

A lot of children who were targeted by bullies lack confidence because of abuse or domestic violence.

Children who aren't confident do not necessarily mean that they have self-confidence are the victims of violence. Abuse encompasses different spectrums. In certain cases parents may be too protective to the point that the child isn't allowed to grow in a normal way. The child may grow up lacking confidence. Two instances of children lacking confidence are Sam as well as Lucas.

Lucas was raised in a home that was abusive. The father of Lucas was an alcohol addict and his mother was a codependent.

When Lucas's father was drunk, which would happen frequently often, he would always hit Lucas or his mother. This caused Lucas believe, from an young age that the man he was "bad. At the end of the day there was something wrong to have his father constantly beat him.

Sam was raised as an all-only child with parents who were more than 40 at the time her birth. Sam was a huge surprise. Her parents gave her everything she could want.

They gave her nothing but the chance to become normal children. While other kids were in the pool, Sam had to be in the house with her parents as she was likely to "catch cold. Sam's mother was so protective and controlled that she continued washing her hair at the swimming pool till she was twelve years old. The reason was that she wanted to ensure that Sam was clean and tidy, and believed it was complicated for Sam to manage it.

When Lucas began going to school, he was making trouble. He would constantly scold other kids in order to unleash his anger on them. He would go home, and become his father's victim. In school, he wasn't popular and was even known to be fearsome. Even though Lucas was a fan of this, he often equated it with admiration.

Others were not worried about Lucas however they frequently was amused by his jokes when Lucas was a snarky child. It was because they were happy that he didn't annoy them.

Sam was having a difficult time in school. Children who were not hers appeared to her like aliens, because she was being constantly in the presence of adults. Because she was never able to rely on herself and was completely incapable of defending herself against the children that were bullies.

It didn't take long before Sam was a school prankster. Sam became the target of bullies who would rather to fight with her instead of with someone who could strike and hit them back. Sam was unable to stand up for herself. The more she ignored the bullies and wished them to go away and leave, the more pathetic she became.

There was Antony. Antony was born into a good home , with parents who were devoted to him, however, they also gave the boy certain responsibilities suitable for his age.

They were determined for Antony to be an independent adult, and not being a child with a lot of attention. They encouraged him through their sports efforts and took him to games. They never told him that he was not good, as did Lucas's father. Or, they helped him at all times as did Sam's parents.

Antony was the clear teacher in the class. The kids would chuckle with Lucas because they were afraid of Antony. However, when the moment arrived to celebrate, it was Antony who everyone was looking forward to at the birthday celebration. The majority of children did not want Lucas at their party, but they invited him because they were scared of losing the boy. They didn't wish to invite Sam to attend their events because they aren't interested in being identified with Sam.

We all know "children are terrible. I've heard adults repeat this over and over in my life. They are. But, guess what is that children are not any more than adults in the sense of being cruel. They're more open about it.

Adults aren't always easy to find, but they have the same rule of thumb. The kids that we have just talked about that we discussed - Antony, Sam and Lucas and their friends could be thought of as the wolves. They are the only wild animals that have an environment with humans and they're just like us. In the wolf pack, there is an alpha male, who is the dominant of the wolves.

In this instance it's Antony. While in this world, inhabited by wolves Antony would be able to use brute force however in the human realm, the intellect typically leads to victories. Humans are animals, however unlike animals, humans can think rationally.

Lucas wasn't the most powerful male, but was simply the team's aggressor. Sam was a lone Wolf. In truth the pack would rather that they did not have Sam and Lucas among them.

The reason is due to the fact that they both aren't confident enough. However, when Lucas becomes older and another more mature child wants to help clean the park with Lucas, Lucas will be reduced to Sam level.

Sam is likely to be the only one throughout his entire life.

It is natural for her to think that people aren't a fan of her due to the experiences she has had, and may do whatever is necessary to create her antipathy to have some control over the disapproval. Her behavior will become ever more strange, to keep other people from her.

With their confidence, Sam and Lucas will not just fit easily into the school setting but also grow into leaders. The confidence can be cultivated into children, and they could be able to start again somewhere else.

The exact same thing was happening in the case of Sam. Sam's teacher told her mom that Sam did not have any friends at school and that she was a lonely person. It was the time Sam was about begin high school. Tomas her mother set up appointments with counselors to help her daughter.

Sam spoke to the counselor that she felt like she didn't have control over her life. Her life was so well-organized and safe that it felt like living inside a glass box. The counselor was stunned by the amount of hair washed.

Fortunately, the parents of Sam took note of the counselor's advice and realized that in trying to shield Sam from harm, they did more than hinder her growth, but caused the loss of her confidence. Sam thought she could take on the world by herself. In the end, Sam began to develop confidence.

The process began by taking tiny steps. First, she washed her hair, pick her own clothes, and decide for herself.

It was a challenge the parents of Sam. They wanted Sam to make a change and stop making mistakes. They explained their job was to let Sam to be an adult with her own independence. Along with making decisions on her own, Sam also began to declare her preferences and likes.

She was a fan of the arts. Her parents had her enroll in art classes to assist her improve her self-esteem and confidence issues, as recommended by their counselor. This assisted Sam to build confidence in herself.

Sam started her first year in high school at a brand new school. In the new school, nobody knew Sam.

It's likely that her former classmates would not recognize her. Even though she was far from being the confident woman she'd eventually be but she was doing extremely well. After several years of being a socially awkward person she was now making friends.

Lucas however, on his part, enrolled in high school but quickly was a minuscule figure. He continued to harass until he was able to harass people who were karate masters.

Lucas was assaulted by a smaller person. He was subsequently sacked of his friends who were no longer afraid of them. Lucas quit school in 11th grade due to the fact that at that point, he was drinking and was not doing any homework.

Antony performed well throughout high school and college. There were highs and lows like every young person however, in the majority of cases Antony was happy and confident.

In the schools of all over the United States, "self-esteem" is a major issue. While some individuals mock the notion that this should not be a problem at any point, some go to an extreme and seek to eradicate any rivalries.

In certain schools, grades are being eliminated in some schools. While children in the younger age group should be encouraged to engage in activities and sports without being judged, the children appear to be stuck in a tense mental state when they believe that just being active could earn them recognition when they grow older.

The majority of school and organised sports help young children to play and gradually prepare them to compete as they get older.

Confidence can be cultivated anytime in a person's life. The sooner it is the more confident.

If you wish to help instill the confidence of your child you have to take the following steps:

Let your child explore various things that they might enjoy including arts and sports, as well as other pursuits.

Make sure your child is given the appropriate chores to complete at home, like making the dinner table.

Don't hit or harass the child. This abusive behaviour can pass on the child. If you notice yourself giving the child nicknames, please apologize and make sure you don't repeat the same thing. If it happens again, seek out therapy to improve your own health for your child.

Do not over-praising the child. This is the exact reverse of those parents who don't ever give praise. When you tell a child that everything he accomplishes is amazing it is prepping them for a fall big time as they enter the world of. You should praise him however, not in all that he does.

Inspire your kid to take on the interests that he or she enjoys. Don't choose the ones you enjoy. Remember, your aim is to create an independent adult. Not a Mini-Yo.

Let your child make mistakes. It's evident that you'd like to safeguard your child. Don't allow the child to burn their hands while cooking and then say, "That will teach you something. However you should not grieve and berate them. There will be mistakes. Letting them make mistakes will allow them to make mistakes and learn from them.

Learn the child's the right behavior and show respect to him or herself, and respect for other people. The most secure people are educated individuals. Manners is not just about the fact that forks or knives should be used, it's equally about having respect for the other.

Give them a sense of independence. There is no need to protect your child. Children naturally want greater independence as they get older. Naturally, you'll be concerned about protecting your child. Make sure you give them the an independence that is appropriate for their age.

The ability to raise children confidently will be the initial step in creating more confident adults around the world.

People who are accountable for their actions are kind to others and do not hesitate to be leaders of the future.

Chapter 2: how to make Self-Consciousness

Self-consciousness is what it sounds like? If we decompose it into its phases it seems harmless. It is, after all, conscious of the self and an essential aspect of humans. Self-consciousness in psychology is an overblown view that we hold about ourselves and what others think of us. Self-consciousness is based upon false beliefs, and can lead us to make assumptions about other people's perceptions. The changes in our behavior reveal our true self and regular behavior. We are all restricted by self-consciousness.

Emotional Exploration

Our emotional world develops by our emotions and experiences. Our actions are the result of our emotions. When you mix these feelings with logic, they result in behavior and actions of humans. How can

25

we look at these emotions? Let's examine the methods that you can use to learn how you feel in the same way that you feel.

Concentrate on breathing to relax your thoughts. Focus your attention on the emotion that is causing your anger, sadness or worry.

Take note of where you feel it physically, such as arms or legs, or even your chest. For some it could be various parts of their body. Concentrate on the areas where feel the most intense emotion. Concentrate on the area that are causing discomfort.

It is possible to feel pain or anxiety when you attempt to confront these emotions. It's okay, it's normal because we've been running towards them throughout the greater portion all of time. Be alert and do not try to get it out. Begin by tagging your curiosity whiskers to this method.

Be aware of the areas of discomfort , and keep your breathing in a calm manner.

Relax your eyes, and visualize you sinking into the depths of these thoughts. In the beginning, your mind may be resistant, but do not force it to. Allow it to rest wherever it is. Then, after one minute, you are able to continue to imagine the sinking in a bit. Repeat this process 3 or 4 instances until you are feeling that you're in the middle of your heart's desires.

In this final phase take your time letting your body breathe through and out at areas of discomfort. Relax and keep your thoughts focussed and not to wander away from the point of discomfort. You can rest at one spot for a few minutes, allowing your mind to expand.

The exercise should be performed frequently, and doing this, you will be able to explore and comprehend your feelings well.

Emotional Consciousness

Self-conscious emotions include shame and guilt, pride and embarrassment. They help us relate to the way people respond to us and our own self-image. We are in a world of social interaction and the perception of others of us is essential for us to progress towards the next level. In school, we are questioned by our teachers. In our professions, we're examined by a panel of experts or even on dates when the other party is deciding whether or not they want to be engaged with you. Today social media and the pressures it creates make us feel more self-conscious and anxious. Technology-driven avenues like Facebook, Twitter, Instagram and a host of others may help us feel more self-conscious, but these feelings are rooted in the human condition.

The voices we hear in our inner world, particularly the critical voice is well-rooted from the time we were children to our mature years. The negative voice will only be influenced by our experiences as adults, but it will never change after that. It is a result of memories of the pain that we endured during our childhood. It isn't necessarily physical or sexual abuse but the little experiences that children experience as kids as they grow older. All of us experience trauma in some form or other and are the reason we feel as if we are different or less important than others. We constantly hear this negative voice within our lives, as we listen to this, the more aware we become. When we understand what self-consciousness means and what it is, let's now look at what it does to us.

When people believe that they are lacking a positive attribute or even a part of their body, they are likely to alter their behavior as a response to self-consciousness. This can cause a person to live a lonely existence or become a person-pleaser to feel loved. This can prevent people from socializing with others. Some people mistake self-consciousness for shyness because they feel embarrassed doing certain things or when they interact. The feelings of self-consciousness can manifest by our body language and how we express ourselves.

The voice of our inner critic creates a sense of self-consciousness, and when we listen to it we can become apathetic and judge ourselves harshly. It is only possible to overcome self-consciousness by recognizing the negative voices and working to counter each day.

Emotional Mechanism

The mental state that is a part of the nervous system triggered by chemical changes related to emotions, thoughts behavior, thoughts, and feelings of pleasure or displeasure. Processing emotional information and behaviour is the function in the brain's amygdala. Numerous studies have demonstrated that plausible circuits relay sensory signals to the amygdalae that aid in emotional processing. Which are five fundamental emotions?

There are a variety of emotions that impact our interactions with each and with each other. You may believe that emotions are the sole source of power decisions, actions and even our perceptions are influenced by emotions. The various types of emotions include:

* Happiness- All of us want to be happy the same way in some way. Happiness is defined as happiness, contentment, satisfaction and overall happiness. This emotion is expressed by body language, facial expressions and a beautiful voice.

* Sadness- Sadness can be described as an emotion that is characterized by frustration, sadness, disinterest and a lowered mood. Everyone experiences this feeling at times however for some the feeling is prolonged and can cause depression. What are the ways to communicate this emotion? Through indolence, a dulled mood tears, withdrawal or even a quiet moment.

* Fear. Fear helps keep us safe from dangerous situations and allows us to stay alive. Some people are sensitive fear, while others seek out situations that can trigger the fear. This emotion can be expressed through our body language. For instance, we open our eyes open, trying to run away from the danger and then awe is the rapid beat of our heart.

* Disgust - This is the feeling of being disgusted. It is expressed through different ways like wiggling our nose, vomiting and turning away from the smell or object that makes us feel disgusted.

* Anger - Anger is an effective negative emotion. It can motivate you to take action in the event of something that is bothering you. What do you do when it happens? Do you throw a frown, look away from the cause of anger, altering your tone to shouting and screaming, hitting or throwing objects.

* Surpriseis an instantaneous emotion that can be negative or positive. This type of emotion manifests itself by raising eyebrows or opening your mouth in a flurry, screaming or gasping. Research shows that surprising facts stick in the memory for a longer period of time.

Other emotionsinclude contentment and relief, shame, amusement, guilt exuberance, embarrassment and pride in accomplishment.

The Deepness of Emotions

The depth of our emotions are the way we perceive and comprehend emotions. What can we do to explore the depths of emotions?

Intensity: We should feel the emotions with full force

Feel the fullness of these feelings within our bodies.

- Substance depth;

Space Depth and time.

What are the traits of those with a keen understanding of the depth of their feelings?

Feeling various emotions, apart from sadness and anger.

They can tell the way they feel.

They are able to distinguish their emotions. This means they are able to discern what emotions they are experiencing, as well as having more than 100 emotions in humans.

They are able to identify the reason for their feelings and what was the reason.

They don't feel ashamed to react to live performances with their own emotions.

Emotions are not always deep. It happens the case when emotions overwhelm people and they don't have any idea of what's happening.

Mindfulness

It's a state of mind in which one is aware of their current moment. It is possible to achieve it through practice, such as meditation. People who are mindful don't dwell on the past and neither do they look forward to the future, but are now. They hold their thoughts and emotions and never consider them to be incorrect or wrong. Let's take a look at the benefits of mindfulness.

* The people who practice mindfulness meditation experience an enhanced working memory capacity.

* They will be able to recognize their feelings and clear their minds.

* They have lower levels of anxiety and a high self-esteem.

Focused and don't have a tendency to react emotionally.

They're focused and attentive.

They are also able to have low stress levels.

They are able to control physical pain.

Are mindfulness-related issues harmful? Every advantage has a drawback which is why mindfulness is an one of them. Let's take a look at the disadvantages.

People who meditate regularly are more prone for false memory.

In mindfulness meditation the participants eliminate their negative thoughts and free their minds from negative thoughts. This practice could the people shed some positive thoughts, which could help strengthen.

People who practice mindfulness are able to avoid the strenuous work and prefer to remain in a state of meditation.

The condition can trigger physical and mental issues like hallucinations, derealization and hallucinations.

Know Yourself

Being aware of yourself as it explains, it is able to recognize your strengths and weaknesses as well as your dreams and desires as well as fears, passions, and desires. What are the advantages of knowing you?

* You'll feel more fulfilled by the freedom to be yourself and express yourself.

* You'll have less internal conflicts as your actions will be consistent with your emotions.

Being aware of yourself can aid you in making the right decisions in your daily life.

* You will develop self-control.

* You'll be able to resist the pressures of society.

* Once you understand yourself, you are conscious of your challenges which can make you more compassionate. It helps you comprehend and be tolerant of the other.

* You live and exhilaratingly live the joys of life.

We ought to consider different ways of knowing our own selves, wouldn't we?

Learn about your persona by reflecting.

Be aware of your values and core beliefs and write them down.

Understand and learn about your body's capabilities in order to establish goals, and be aware of your limitations.

Keep a journal each day to think about your own life.

Know your strengths and weaknesses.

Aim for a purpose and have a goal in your the world of.

Cultural Exploration

There are many cultures across the world, and these play an important role in shaping our self-confidence. Our culture was ingrained in us as we were children and their roots are deeply rooted. Many people have looked into other culturesand have led them to a greater understanding of how they perceive themselves. Certain cultures may influence our self-esteem negatively, as well as other positive aspects. In certain culture, women are considered to be a burden and treated as inferior humans. They are not allowed to express their opinion regarding issues that concern their lives and the society. They are not allowed to express their thoughts. From their childhood to adulthood, society works to destroy their self-confidence and self-esteem. This creates a negative image of oneself from a young age, while those who rule these cultures are ego-driven and act as if they are gods. It is important to stay aware of our culture as it is vital however, we shouldn't feel inadequate because of certain cultures that we have no clue about their origins. Being aware of our culture is a process that begins as an individual, and then becomes a part of a larger group. Our cultural traditions should be a uniting force but not define us.

Highlighting Strengths

It is crucial to identify our strengths so that we can get the most out of our abilities. What do you know about your strengths? Your strengths are the things that make you feel more comfortable and could cause others problems. Your strengths should be utilized to the maximum extent possible since that will give you an edge in your competition. Knowing your strengths is similar to having a sense of value that makes you aware of your strengths. If you recognize your strengths, it helps you understand your strengths and the way you perform. Why should we be focusing upon our weaknesses?

It can help you feel more positive feelings.

The act of highlighting your strengths can boost confidence in yourself.

By making the most of our strengths we are more efficient.

Finding Blind Spots

We may not be aware of the role we play in the causes of our issues. We all have blind spots and it's easier to see these in other people than our own. Blind spots are the weaknesses within our own that keep us from fulfilling our full potential. It is much easier to see the blind spots of others than our own. Everyone of us has to look at ourselves from another's perspective. It's the first step to self-consciousness. Blind spots are like setting up cameras in our lives to see how our actions affect issues we wish to fix. It provides us with the full picture of what we need to do to take action instead of blame other people.

Have you noticed blind spots? I know that I've said that we all have blind spots But do you know where your blindspots are? Recognizing those blind spots can be a difficult task; it's an attack on denial. Denial is more damaging than ignorance. It's the capacity to discern the facts and then not let it to enter our minds. Certain information that is scary or troubling can cause us to have blind areas. This is the mind's way to safeguard us. Finding your blind spots similar to chasing the wind. Can you catch it? It's not easy however the great thing is the blind spot leaves tracks. These tracks are a result of repeated life experiences that are hard to be able to explain. A few examples include:

You are always in similar relationships, despite your people in the relationship being different.

Your destiny is never changing.

People will always be describing you in a way you're not.

How can you rid yourself of those blind spots?

If you are able to track frequent events in your daily life, you may have blind spots. The easiest method to remove these is to pay attention. It is not necessary to be harsh on yourself. Be gentle with yourself and allow greater consciousness. Ask yourself these questions to seek help.

What am I afraid to ask?

What is it I find it challenging to understand?

What am I noticing in my head?

The answers that pop up in your thoughts are evidence of an important step toward self-awareness, be gentle and patient with yourself as you make breakthroughs. These efforts can be beneficial for your self-awareness. But the most effective approach is to ask for feedback from your family members and family. Honest feedback is important and could save you lots of time.

Feedback

Feedback is crucial for growth and change; however, what matters is how you manage it. Certain feedbacks can hurt you or even make you. Everyone hates getting negative feedback and we all respond differently to negative feedback. Our reactions could be negative or right, but the majority of us do not know the right answer.

Constructive feedback is based from observations. The focus is on a particular problem and is specific. There are four kinds of feedback.

"*" Positive validates the validity of past behaviour. It focuses on behavior that is successful that we can continue to follow.

Negative feedback- Corrects annotations about behavior from the past. It examines the unproductive action that is to be fixed and not repeatable.

* Negative feed-forward - Corrects annotations about the behavior that will occur in the near future. It examines the behavior that we need to be avoiding in the near future.

Positive feed-forward- Validates comments about the future behavior. It is focused on behaviors that can enhance future performance.

If we hear feedback from our family members and friends It can be a bit scary for us all. The harsh feedback is difficult to process, and the majority of us would prefer to escape and hide rather than confront the issue. The harsh feedback can make us feel uncomfortable, and they can damage certain people's confidence. How do you deal with difficult feedback? Utilize the following strategies to manage it like an expert you are.

Find the positive within it.

Even in the most harsh criticism there's positive aspects to it. Seek it out and use it to boost your self-confidence. When you're the target or subject of critique, you feelings may prevent you from looking at the larger perspective. You can, however, consult a trusted friend family member if they believe there is any truth to the criticism. If the answer is yes it is time to work on making an improvement for tomorrow.

See the bigger picture; the truth

The majority of us see criticism as negative because we interpret it the criticism as a threat to us. However, this is far from the reality. Feedback is not about the person you are, but about your performance. It is best to not internalize feedback to damage our self-esteem, but rather take it in and discover the truth.

Take a look at the origin

Prior to reacting to feedback, it's best to investigate the source. Does it come from a person who has enough information about the issue at hand, and what the motives of the person are.

Walk away

In certain instances there are instances where criticism is not intended for our benefit. Certain people are naturally nasty. If the feedback is an unintentional negative comment intended to cause harm, then consider taking a step or two back for at most two minutes. It's not like I'm suggesting you hide, this is designed to make you think more clear and not be influenced by your feelings. Being angry won't aid you. The best way to resolve the issue is by being calm and honest. Don't forget that words of slander can cause a negative response.

Move on

Remorse, rectify the mistake And then continue.

You should be curious.

Do not get offended due to negative feedback, but instead, find out the reason behind it by honest dialogue with the person you disagree with.

Try to imagine yourself in the shoes of their characters

Try to walk in someone else's in their shoes and try to understand the other person's perspective. Consider things from their point of view and consider if they are trying to hurt or help you. When you think about that there is a good chance that you'll be able to determine the best way to respond.

There is no way to ignore negative feedback, but we can train ourselves to manage it. Feedback is essential as it aids us in growing and improve our self-esteem. Remember, we're part of this journey together. Many of us have been theretoo.

Chapter 3: elegant Lenses Set

"If you want to be happy, keep in mind that the need to release inspires energy and hope," declares Andrew Carnegie. However, the ability of the person who has the most trouble in achieving the goals will cease since you are not having any issues in the way you conduct yourself in conflict with others. The belief that you have in yourself and your abilities is all you require to accomplish your goals. That's why Devers declared: "To keep your dreams to come to life. Know that it will require you to be successful what you believe in. faith can be based on the vision, dedication as well as support and commitment. Keep in mind that everything can be achieved by those who believe in themselves. I believe in the power to succeed and to focus on the things you love. and the luck that is to come and he will never do things that you don't think of that your passion is strong and the faith of the masses has a high chance of being able to achieve it is of major importance to the future of your hands. Take everything in the moment of luck's influence. If you're content and relaxed it will not be a problem for anyone else. the. emotional turmoil has brought the pain of the surroundings of our lives: the importance of justice is a bit for humans, Bill Coping states that "the problem is in the fact that one can live your all day running around the countryside, but never making a move."

Brian Tracy wants you to be aware the fact that "they seem to feed the success of the oven." People who do not show and enjoy triumph over us. This was the view in the case of Marco Tullio Marden, he has said that he was right: "Those who had done great things in the eyes were, as we have noted, that the way might be thought." The men that are happy have done the amazing work that will be revealed to you.

It made sure that those who don't make sense, and made Mauris be miserable. Men don't get bored with their daily life. Lou Holtz, who unrolled: "If you get tired of life and you don't have: early in the morning early to look, and all with a burning desire to do something, whose will is not good enough" there's anything you are not able to achieve your goals that you don't have other than life's challenges for you. "Objectives. We can not say what you can do to inspire them. We can not say what we do when we can not trust him. I can not say what should be done with them", Jim Rohn states. So, there is not a time to wait. It is the time to confront the enemy, in a cruel hurt, and offer your life with an appeal to the world and within a short period of time it will all be well for you. If you're looking to dream and dream, do it with a powerful voice.

"It should never be easy to divide. What is needed to limit the disadvantages of time," claims Michael Phelps? Don't be afraid of having to limit your personal space. The bottom line is that there's no limitation. Ted Turner wants to know the "purpose." The way you have lived your life has always been. "Your goals are a problem. This isn't the same as if many people suffer from recent catastrophes have suffered in the past. You cannot achieve what you think as feasible. "What is the root cause for the delays? Goals are essential to the success of your strategy. It is enough to present the case that there's no harm if you wish to live life to its highest degree. Jim Rohn says," If you do not create your life. Effective, the plan will likely. You've planned it, and it's not much. but in the case of Pablo Picasso, he rightly stated that the goals must be accomplished through a political system that is based on the conviction that we should act with determination. The only other method of prosperity. This way the consumer is not able to achieve any goals; he's taken the route of inability.

Rabindranath Tagore has said that the plan "will rise since the sky is hidden to your sight. Pharaoh, the dream of resting in the depths. The aim is only placed in prison. I'm not sure what could hinder your decision. "When you modify your thinking and think differently, you will change things around, "said Steve Maraboli. Invariably. The creation of a powerful positive attitude. In the words of Jill Koenig," objective to determine if it's worthwhile to wait for it to be achieved is not possible in daily life. "For this to happen, Steve Garvey says: "It is important to establish some goalsthat are not achievable. If you can, because it takes an enormous amount of work and that the outcome isn't the goal of the thinking process, then something less could be stuck in the potential and ability. Additionally, Sid Cesar, wants you to learn about his life ", like the aliquot among those who say he is the soul, to live and enjoy things about you." This is not to gain the joy of being full to God that's at work or is difficult to establish. It's not shocking; Orison Marden stated "that some of you've performed amazing things in order that your eyes are being reflected back into the space that it was born and then was visible. "In short the goal is to gamble a huge and exciting life.

In the words of Norman Gould, "that all men have a happy end. The fact that no one should be denied that if they do I'm not sure where to go to get whatever they wish, because each soul who doesn't come ahead of itself otherwise, it will be swept away by the waves of depression and disorientation. An idea to put them in the proper direction for us, and to keep the faith of us. Benjamin Mays said: "The tragic nature of life doesn't involve the final destination. The goals that must be fulfilled and the instances where they don't. These are the main goals of living. If one's wheel is spinning in their soul is spinning, and who does not, it is because they're at a minimum, leading an active daily life that is centered on prayer. In the end, as M. Brown explained, "if you designate your goals with all of them to follow, and careful consideration, how you can achieve it, gives you a gift, that the places are ashamed." Canon is right to say, "We must not have the same conversation, or even discuss the subject, or to be a part of the process of consulting procedure. If you do to the next level, I don't know which areas you don't have it. Since the majority of those who've made suggestions is beautiful, it's not necessary for these resolutions to be taken down. Based on these three, Brad Stulberg must be acknowledged that "the procedure that determines whether it is a good idea to be to believe that it's external borders and also that the system of persecution is among the most desirable aspects of human nature. "Do not attempt to stifle it. It's the purpose of the naive in pursuing the goals in a manner that is not managed and defended with scrupulous integrity.

"For each day, there is a connection; one of them is necessary, decisions, and training. There are two elements of the same currency, so to speak: those called to" define objectives "and" set goals. " It is possible to differentiate from one another, so that the other is not of any useful. This is why it is essential to evaluate the whole your hands and work hard and achieve the goals. The reason it is due to specific goals The second Gavin Bird ", which is a reference to some of my priests and the anger is still there. Shields, although challenging to attain according to their view, have integrity that is scrupulous is possible to determine. As per Zig Ziglar, "to achieve it, it's not as important are the goals that need to be met," accordingly, according to Brian Tracy, "if you would like, and I'll give you the rage of your potential as well as unlocking it, it has to be given to the governor that used to be in daily life, and who suggested that you can perform. "Pe It's complicated, but it's not difficult to accomplish. Whatever you do is focused on achieving happiness for your life, yourself, as well as the whole region. It is not clear that the image is clearly defined in its cost. We frequently consider what could be accomplished, but there are no restrictions and if they are not addressed Similar to Michael Phelps, select targets which are "disadvantages." Set performance goals that do not even a little either, or are not, and do not require the efforts of the people who want to join you.

"People are not able to achieve greater goals, which is why they're not defined. They aren't always cruel adversaries they are being presented as reliable and swift rescue. Where do they go? winners will tell you how they'll do as they take part in the fight, "said Denis Waitley. Setting goals is not enough to make them clear. These monsters will be on the steps you must take in order to accomplish these goals. Make a list of your goals that are not forgotten when you first try. Mark Hansen's suggestions and savings on your goal and the paper will help you start the process to become the individual you would like to be. Give your future in good hands, yours. There's no way to fulfill to fulfill a goal you do not even know about. If the written statement is not in the document it is difficult to discern the need to pay particular attention to what is in order to reach your goals one by one. I'm reminded of "all is well that purpose. No one should be given, if not the one who knows, who wants to go, if he wants, and do what is not. "-- Peale, Norman said. Therefore, even if they don't know the right course of action when they do not meet the established goals John Pulsifer's decision is not a factor in what is "his life and the lives of the people around him" for the rest of his life.

As per Jack Canfield, "it does not matter how positive your attitude is to make people feel happy about the reasons for things that are still alive. The past was not always so good. the issues that we've seen here in our country of the United States tend to the wrongs of the past as does the behavior that is a result of the actions of those closest to them should be their goals and also a component of their hospitality, whether as representatives or administrative staff. "Before the slaughter of being ignorant the Americans were extremely compassionate and determined to look forward. Find out what you can do by being positive and doesn't affect the problems that will arise in your life. Are you worried regarding the very same individuals you can't solve. Set goals that will solve human problems. When we make progress and the world celebrates, everyone will rejoice. So, when peacetime comes around there is a saying the following quote from Michael Korda: "We need to establish ourselves more and more easily." It's not surprising to find that Alberti V. Haller is cited"If you'd like to live a fulfilled life and in the end, there are people. "Nothing will influence your life other than set goals. When you look back at the prior goals it was your responsibility to improve. The capacity to let me go with the truth is your choice It is in your capabilities. Waste is to accomplish anything, and you can achieve if the goals are set to pursue.

"It's tougher than being at the top of the hill. The quest for new goals never ends. -- Pat Summitt said many attempts to boost happiness throughout the day. Continue to run before finding fresh ideas. Try to find new avenues each day, and if you know someone who has an impact on your life, they should perform better than they did, not worse and apply it to their way of thinking. However, I've got a solution to many of the issues that face humanity, and I'm able to locate it, and find out if there are any surprising traits that remain and persist regardless of the fact that everyone is gets a second Nightingale, "success is not enough to be considered a breakthrough or at the end." In this way, the idea of success is emphasized. Each operation must be a full-time successes. There is more to you. If you follow my advice that one thing is not possible to do. Goals for you to do it: let you retreating to them, and concentrate on, and success: and for you the other person, it's theirs. Rhode Island, the rope that is at the end of the tunnel was gone It is never heavy such as just a bit of effort and perseverance, you can achieve.

"The concept isn't any more appealing in the short run. I'm sure those who took their initiative and also to enhance the power of people, and the third ..." second. Seth to argue that you shouldn't be like the people who are striving to live a life without any goals. It's amusing in the first place but, when it comes to end, it's the death of the tire. This is not possible without Aliquip's success. Aliquip. This could result in less effective situations. "Sometimes we thank God we thank God for the progress we've made and provides us with physical and mental strength. We pray for joy We increase the possibility of greater endurance, or, if we wish us to grow the amount of joy we feel with the grace God has given us. Trust It provides us with the idea that we must are striving to reach the highest standards, "says David Bednar'. The men are the responsibility of us in our lives. It is our responsibility to act with a sense of humour and who can say that is not possible to accomplish their goals and release the enemy, using the brutal present, and not. This was not done to improve the capabilities of all sides and it is not something we can do when they're not committed to do it with force. Then he looks at you? The outcome is not a pleasant one for the proposal one of them.

Chapter 4: Factors That concern Grit

We have discussed earlier that factors such as ability, or even interest and desire can drive a person's desire to be tough. But, as we've seen it isn't enough and hasn't proven to suffice and has never been. Since the last time, many people depend on their abilities in a way that isn't right and put huge amounts of weight on it, believing that it will take care of them. Ability can be cultivated naturally by doing specific exercises. What it does is it helps in making flawlessness a less join. It eases the burden of work that is difficult, but it doesn't eliminate the primary need.

The ability should never be traded in exchange for tough work or the ability to work hard. The various factors that affect determination and grit are influenced by age. While the expression, "the older you grow, the more intelligent you will become' isn't a straight-forward statement however, it is true that aging affects the quality of grit in a way.

It's also possible that the patterns of aging are not related to changing grit generation by generation. What the data could be indicating is the method by that individuals change after a certain period of. My understanding and stories of grit-loving gurus such as Jeff Gettleman and Bob Mankoff suggest that, in fact the grit we develop is when we understand our theories of life and discover ways to get rid of ourselves from discontent and rejection and discover the distinction between small-level goals that need to be discarded quickly and the more substantial higher-level goals demand more dedication. The development narrative is that we increase the threshold of commitment and interest over the long term as we grow more established.

Children are being manipulated by the idea that they're frequently on the globe to play. Growing older doesn't cause a person to become more grizzled and sassy, but rather gives an individual a more stable sense of direction. The feeling is that one must be trying to make up for lost time, and they realize that they should stop playing about with their lives.

Social exposure: the social environments one is raised in is a major factor that determines the grit of people. This is the role of nurture and how an individual develops. A person who was raised in a gang of thieves is more likely to end up as the criminal. This is due to the fact that people frequently use their surroundings to determine their identity. This is not a firm idea since there are people who have fought the effects of genetics, but it's a significant element. Each society is unique and has its own value. This is the reason why certain societies excel in certain areas over others.

Consistency: As of late, presented an introductory talk on grit students of the Wharton School of Business. Even after I had removed my notes off the stage an aspiring business professional ran to the podium to introduce himself.

He was brimming with the energy and vitality which makes talking to children so enjoyable. With enthusiasm, he shared with me an account that was that was meant to show his massive strength. In the previous year, he had raised a large amount of money for his business venture and had gone to extreme the lengths necessary to accomplish this and even pulling a few all-nighters along the way.

I was awestruck and told the same. However, I was quick to mention that the all-nighters tend to be more about endurance than strength. "Along these lines, in case you're chipping away at that venture with a similar vitality in a year or two, email me. I can say more regarding your grit at that point."

He was puzzled. "Indeed, I probably won't be taking a shot at something very related in a couple of years."

I responded, "I'm not saying you're incorrect, but the majority of stories that seem positive at first are a complete failure. A lot of brilliant strategies are discarded in the may.

"Okay, so perhaps this specific start-up won't be what you're looking at in the long run. In case you're not working in a similar industry, in the event that you're on to some absolutely inconsequential of interest, at that point I don't know if your story shows grit."

"That is to say, remain in one company?" He asked.

"Not really. Skipping around starting with one sort of interest then onto the next, from one range of abilities to an extraordinary one; that is not what gritty individuals do."

"In any case, imagine a scenario where I move around a great deal and, while I'm doing that, I still work hard?"

"Grit isn't simply buckling down. That is just a piece of it."

Pause.

"Why?"

"For a certain something, there are no alternate routes to greatness. Growing genuine ability, making sense of extremely difficult issues, everything requires some investment--longer than the vast majority of envisioning. And afterward, you must apply those aptitudes and produce products or administrations that are significant to individuals. 'Rome wasn't built in a day'."

He was listening and I decided to continue.

"Furthermore, here's an extremely significant thing. Grit is tied in with taking a shot at something you care about so much that you're willing to remain faithful to it."

"It's doing what you love. I get that."

"Correct, it's doing what you love, yet not simply falling in love but sticking to love through the long haul."

The New Science: Newton's original law "a body at rest tends to stay at rest and a body in motion tends to stay in motion unless acted on by a net external force". New knowledge is an external force, which shifts and aligns our path throughout our lives.

One reason for why you change is because we learn to master things we were unaware of before. For instance, we could find out through experience that trading in one career aspiration to pursue another one isn't fulfilling. This is exactly what been my experience in my 20s. Following the start of a charitable event, I found that being a "promising newbie can be enjoyable, but becoming a true master is infinitely more rewarding. I also learned that lengthy periods of hard work are frequently mistaken for the natural abilities and that the power of energy is just as important as consistency to achieve world-class excellence. What is consistent is that it builds skill, and should be improved. A lot of skilled people have their skills in a sloppy manner. It is possible to say that they are confident in the spontaneity that their talents evoke. It is important to realize that we are the things we constantly do.

Similar to this we are taught, as the author John Irving did, that "to do anything truly well, you need to overextend yourself," to appreciate the fact that "in accomplishing something, again and again, something that was never characteristic turns out to be practically natural," and lastly, you are able to do work consistently "doesn't come from nowhere."

Apart from bits of information about human nature What else can we learn that is changing as you age?

What changes, I believe is our circumstances. As we become mature individuals, we're challenged to adapt to new conditions. We are offered our first position. We may get hitched. As our parents age as the requirement to take after them comes into play. Infrequently, the new situations force us to be unique contrary to our normal routine. Furthermore, there is none of us more adaptable than ours as we evolve. We adjust to our environment.

We alter when we need to. It is the necessity that is the source of invention.

Here's a model of a lesser caliber. In one way or the other my most beautiful newborn daughter, Lucy was born at 3 without being able to figure out what to do with the toilet. My spouse and I had put in an extremely successful effort to induce or coax her to quit using diapers. We'd read every book and tried to carry out each of these activities. With no results Lucy's way of thinking appeared to be more grounded than ours.

A few days after her birthday party, Lucy changed preschool homerooms and moved from the baby study room in which the majority of kids were still wearing diapers. She moved to the "big children's study hall with no changing table. When I first dropped Lucy out of the old room her eyes were widening, as she pondered the new situation with a bit of apprehension--I believe--and possibly wish she was in her room in which she'd grown accustomed.

I'll never forget getting Lucy the next evening. She smiled at me and said she'd used the toilet. After that, in large numbers of words she informed me that she was done with diapers. In addition she was. Potty training took place in one moment.

How?

As children lined up to use the toilet, she was able to see how the system operated and she followed the exact procedure. She came up with a way to accomplish what she had to accomplish.

Bernie Noe, the director of the Lakeside School in Seattle, told the story of his daughter. It exemplifies the developmental standard perfectly. The family of Noe lives close by and, as a young child his daughter was always late to school. One summer, the girl discovered a brand new job line that was folding clothes at the nearby American Eagle. The first day she started her supervisory head said, "Gracious, coincidentally, the first occasion when you're late, you're terminated." The employee was stunned. What if she had an opportunity to re-evaluate her mistake? All her life, she'd experienced forbearance understanding, compassion, and new opportunities.

What was the issue?

"It was stunning," Noe said. "Literally, it was the most prompt conduct change I've seen her make." Then, the daughter set two alarms to make sure she was on time or on time, in a job where tardiness was not tolerated. As a supervisor tasked with guiding children towards growth, Noe thinks about his ability to accomplish this to a extent. "In case you're a business, you couldn't care less whether a child believes they're extraordinary. What you care about is 'Would you be able to deliver? If you can't do this, hello, we don't have any need for you'." In the field of child development, tutors do not have the freedom to work this way.

The development guideline that comes to, according to me is this. After a certain period we master life lessons that we can recall and adapt it to the ever-changing demands of our environment. As time passes, more effective methods to think and act become routine. It comes to a point where we are unable to recall our younger self. We've adapted and the adjustments have become more pronounced until the character we have become, that persona we consider ourselves to be, has developed. We've developed.

When taken together, the data I've collected on grit and age is backed by two different stories. One of them says that our grit changes over time as part of the social context when we are growing up. Another version says we become more grittier as grow older. Both are possible however I am in doubt as to whether they are. In any event this image reveals the fact that grit can't be fixed completely.

Other factors influence the growth of grit among individuals.

I receive letters and messages from people who wish they had more determination. They are sad that they haven't stuck with something long enough to become proficient at it. They are convinced that they have lost their talents. They are in desperate need of a long-term purpose and need to search for that goal with a lot of determination and interest.

In any event they don't have the slightest idea of the best place to begin.

An excellent place to begin is to consider the present situation. If you're not as shrewd as you could be, ask yourself what the reason.

The most obvious response that people might think of is the following "I think I'm just a lazy bum." There's a different one: "I'm only a quitter."

On the contrary: "I'm inherently unequipped for staying with things."

The answers to all of them I'm convinced that aren't true.

If people fall out of things, they usually have an excuse or excuse. They do it for a variety of reasons. The four factors could be circling through your mind before you decide to quit:

"I'm exhausted."

"The exertion isn't justified, in light of potential benefits."

"This isn't essential to me."

"I can't do this, so I should surrender."

When these statements are put into a moral framework, there's much wrong with it. The way I want to say in this section the paragons of grit and goals are also. The more affluent the goal being referred to and the more stubbornly they are in controlling the process. Paragons of grit aren't able to use compasses to guide their decisions: in relation to one thing of them, a crucial factor that is the basis of almost all they do, the gritty doesn't make statements similar to those mentioned above.

The majority of the information I've gathered about the development of grit stems from speaking with people who embody the traits of curiosity and perseverance. I've put bits of these discussions throughout the book in hopes to let you peek into the mind and soul of a grit guru and determine if there's a belief, mentality or inclination to emulate.

These stories of grit complement the more systematic qualitative investigations I've made at places such as West Point and the National Spelling Bee. Together, these investigations reveal the mental resources that create the grit paragons to all intents and reasons. Four of them are. They will take on each of the buzz-executioners listed in the previous paragraph, and can create, over through the decades, particular demand.

The first step is to get interested. The first step is to get an enjoyment from the work you do. Every person I've met has highlighted aspects of their job that they enjoy of their daily tasks that they hate. They're in awe of their jobs and careers.

With a constant excitement and positive outlook they shout, "I love what I do!"

The next step is discipline practicing. A type of focus is day-to control of trying to make improvements over the previous day's performance. After you've discovered enthusiasm for something then you must commit yourself to the type of intense, full-hearted, challenging skill-building that leads to proficiency. Focus on your weaknesses and do the same thing over and over for a lengthy period of time, day after day after day. Being tough is to challenge poor attitudes. "Whatever it takes, I need to improve!" is a stumbling block to any grit-loving character regardless of their particular focus, or how great they have become. Thus, it is imperative to practice regardless of emotions or circumstance. It is important to remember that just like everything else in life, unguarded extremes could eventually lead to self-destruction.

The third one is the purpose. The energy of purpose creates the belief that what you do is important. For many , an curiosity without purpose is impossible to sustain over the course of their lives. It is essential that you define your work as fascinating and also a part of the well-being of other people. For a couple of years an individual, the sense of direction is evident early. For others individuals, the motivation to serve others is heightened after the growth of curiosity and prolonged periods of practice. In any event, if you are making models of grit constantly Let me know if "My work is significant, both to me and to other people."

Additionally, it is a thing which never fails to keep you going regardless of the difficulty. The book I am writing about speak about it in terms of research in practice, a sense of purpose, and a desire to succeed However, I do hope that it doesn't define the final stage of determination. From the very beginning as much as is feasible, it's important to determine the best way to stand up when things get difficult or when we are faced with doubts. At different levels, in enormous ways, we get wrecked. If we are down, grit suffers. If we stand up Grit wins.

Without the assistance of an analyst such as me, you might have figured out the meaning of grit on your own. It is possible that you have a strong and persistent curiosity, a fervent desire to take the test consistently as well as a refined sense that you are in the right direction, as well as a slender faith in your ability to stand up to ensure any affliction that could sink. If this is the case, then you're close to being in the top gear!

If you're not as strong as you would like to become, this moment, there's something to be found in the sections that follow. As with piano and math it is possible to become proficient by utilizing the brain science of gritty on its own, however having a bit of direction can help tremendously.

The four mental sources of desire, practice and hope do not exist. You either have it or do not. You can determine the best way to discover, develop and expand your talents. You can develop the desire to be disciplined. You will develop a sense of direction and meaning. Additionally, you can teach yourself to believe in. You can improve your grit from front to the back. If you'd like to learn howto develop your grit, read this article.

Chapter 5: public Anxiety

What Is Social Anxiety

The feeling of social anxiety can be described as a common feeling of anxiety when you're in a social context. It's a psychological and a medical problem However, there are strategies to manage this. Fear can make you be cautious about anything that can disrupt your daily routine. You'll experience the effects of intense stress throughout the day when you suffer from a condition known as social anxiety. You can develop the ability to be comfortable and ways to improve your ability to communicate with others. Social anxiety affects anyone regardless of age and causes people to be self-conscious.

It is normal to worry that those who judge you negatively which can make you feel inadequate and sometimes depression could strike you. You'll have the challenge of focusing your entire attention on yourself when you are in a social situation. Heart rate along with your breathing rate, will rise in response to stress, which is an emotional response that helps prepare for the event that you're about to take on. Anxiety can be to the point of making your sleepless nights, and fatigue. Stress is not just a cause of harm to your body, but it can also bring benefits of it. A brief period of stress can help boost your immune system.

Where It Comes From

Social anxiety isn't the result of unidentified illness that appears from nowhere. There are three main causes that can cause social anxiety and they're:

It's in Your Genes

Sometimes, it's just a matter of anxiety about social situations, fear of crowds, anxiety about public speaking, anxiety or tension due to the fact that it is a trait that runs through your family. People who inherit social anxiety aren't the only ones around 25% of their family members are suffering from this same issue. Genes play a crucial part in shaping the personality and character of a person which includes social anxiety. Does that mean that you are hopeless? It's not! You are able to manage your anxiety. I'll show you how later.

It's How You Were Raised

While it's easy to attribute your parent's behavior for anxiety you experience but it's not always an effective solution since parents want the most beneficial for their children and therefore take steps to ensure the same. In the event that your parents are over cautious, or overly controlling, or did not provide you with an outline of the steps for living a fulfilled life, you could be suffering from anxiety over social situations.

It's Because Of Some Trauma

It's never been more complex, and so mysterious. What we experience today may were not happening fifty or sixty years ago. If you were to ask an older person what is social anxiety and they'd likely not know how to respond! The world of today is brimming with unanticipated threats, increasing costs of living, violent incidents, crimes and more. The world we live in can make a healthy person subject to social anxieties.

Anxiety in Teenagers

Strategies to deal with Social Anxiety

Your teenage son is a mysterious person living in your home. Hormones have been driving them insane for a while and they sometimes want to speak to you, but at times they aren't. Simply put, it's difficult to comprehend the mind of teenagers and comprehend the state of it. They're beginning to meet and they're doing well at school, engaged in sports, and they might even have the job of their dreams. All of these are falling on your teenager, however they're not comfortable enough to talk about it with you. And even although you'd like to assist them, it can cause you to feel uncomfortable which is why you keep it to yourself.

Watch for changes in your emotional state

Certain teenagers might experience extreme worry, while other teens may display other signs, such as being "keyed up," feeling in a state of anxiety, being extremely upset and irritable, inability to concentrate or concentrating, or irritability, or inexplicably loud outbursts. It is possible that they do not have control over certain problems, which is why it's crucial to keep the lines of communication open when you begin to be noticing changes in your child.

Pay attention to social changes

Anxiety can cause stress on the relationships of your teenaged. Even if your child was at one time a social butterfly it's important to note any sudden changes in their social interaction. If they begin to withdraw from their friends from the usual or avoid activities outside of school or are unable to communicate with others or are spending longer in solitude then it could be the right an appropriate time to discuss with them and find out whether they are experiencing something. This could indicate a symptom of a phase however it could also be anxiety.

Physical changes

Most of the time it is the case that there are changes in the physical manifestations of your teenager there is a chance that it's something more than a cold, however it could be the beginning of something more severe. If they're suffering from headaches that are getting more frequent stomach issues, unanswered discomforts and aches, excessive fatigue, feeling not good without a medical reason or changes to your eating routine, it could be an indication that they're experiencing physical changes caused by a rise in anxiety. Visit a doctor if think this is an option to help your teenager receive the nutritional assistance that they may require.

Sleep patterns are changing

It is suggested that teens are getting between 8 and 10 hours of sleep each night. They should turn off their screens for 30 minutes before bedtime to ensure that their minds are able to close off. It's normal to have social engagements, homework and other the like to play a part in the sleep habits of teenagers. However, when you notice an increase in problems with your teenager getting sleepy, staying in bed, and not feeling rested after 8-10 hours or having more vivid nightmares, it could be your teenager's social position isn't the primary cause for the sleep issues. You can try an alternative to melatonin or make sleep rituals for them. However, when it becomes too much of a concern, you should seek medical assistance.

Schoolwork is not always the best.

Since anxiety can impact everything from diet to sleep It is likely that, with these contributing factors, your child may be struggling in school due to their anxiety. Most of the time anxiety makes kids be absent from school due to anxiety about being around other people. One thing to be aware of with your child is significant increases in the grades of your child, frequent absences from assignments, saying that they are overwhelmed by the work load and putting off projects and homework more than normal.

It's possible that your child has been experiencing anxiety for a while , but has not shared this information with you. They might not be able handle the data or may be ashamed of the situation. You must ensure that you are making sure that you are in constant contact with your child. Sometimes, it can be difficult to get them to open up Here are some suggestions for achieving this:

Empathize

Although your teenager wants to become independent, they need to feel validated and respected. If your child is the one to come up with the idea that something is absurd or even illogical, that's an opportunity to demonstrate that you can understand as you once walked in the same position. Show them that you understand your feelings and actually want to help them through whatever they're experiencing. It's not bad to let them see that you're cool as well.

Relate

Inform your child that they're not alone in this. Tell them about any issue you're experiencing that could be directly related to their situation. When you openly discuss the struggles you have and anxieties with them, it could enable them to talk to you too. Make them feel like you are someone who understands their struggles and dispel the idea that teenagers can never understand what they're experiencing.

Ask

If your child seems having a hard time, inquire about what's going on. Inform them that regardless of the circumstance they are able to talk with you. It is important to let them know that whatever they can talk to you and you'll keep your cool and not be judgmental of them. Judging them is just as harmful as the fear itself. They must be aware that they have the ability to reach out to you at times when the stress they're facing are just too difficult to bear.

Most important for you to do as a parent with your child this moment is make them aware that this is normal. Make sure they know that they're not "crazy" because right now there's a possibility that they they could be. They don't know the issues that are affecting them, and they require some understanding. Make sure you're making sure to remind them as often as you can that you're willing to talk openly about things they require to talk about and that there's no judgement in the process. Reducing the stress cycle early will make it easier to be a natural teenagers for them.

Chapter 6: Your True Self?

We all have a variety of views, opinions and beliefs regarding ourselves and others as well. We use our opinions and perceptions to make predictions and judgements regarding the reasons why people behave in certain ways. If someone you don't recognize as a person such as a friend or colleague, could be anyone else, starts screaming or says something in anger You will either distrust this person and believe that the person has an uncontrollable temper or is always in a state of anger. Another way to think about it could be that the person may be suffering from stress or frustration. If you think this way it is likely to forgive them.

This means that there will be times in which you believe your actions as a person reflect the circumstances they are living in or the state of mind they are in. There are instances when you're convinced to believe that everything an individual does is a reflection of their true self.

A lot of psychologists have taken an keen interest in studying the characteristics that we believe to be part of a person's authentic self. In addition, they attempted to grasp how the true self affects the behavior of an individual as well as their interactions with others.

In general terms If we think about our personal identity or the self-reality of other people What traits and characteristics do we believe it has?

One of the most fascinating aspects of the self that is real is that it resembles the form of a thought or belief that is common across all different cultures.

This implies that the diverse aspects and aspects of the self's true nature were thought about and studied by various people all over the earth.

The most important two assumptions are that a person's real self is likely to be moral and ethical. Thus, when individuals change their lifestyles and behaviors They are likely to be viewed to be acting in line with their true self-image whenever they switch from undesirable actions to acting morally and reverse. This is the reason the moment someone stops drinking alcohol, as an example it is viewed as revealing their true self evident by their actions. On the other hand, anyone who begins drinking alcohol is viewed as hiding their true identity.

This is why we believe that any person is likely to transform positively as time passes regardless of whether their previous life was full of immoral and unrighteous actions. This means that we cannot determine if someone is an evil person. We are inclined to believe that every person's inner self is hidden morality that could be revealed and inspire them to perform righteous actions in the upcoming period.

The other interesting aspect about the real self is that the way we think believe about ourselves and about other people's real self aren't different. The beliefs and the thoughts we hold differ in how we perceive our motives and intentions in comparison to individuals who belong to another group than we do. We frequently think that we're morally upright and have higher moral standards as compared to people belonging to different groups. However, we also occasionally believe that members of different groups are moral and moral individuals in their own right.

Does the concept of real self-importance really that important?

This notion is important. Being true to yourself affects the judgements of people around you regarding the actions that provide meaning to your life. One who puts in the effort to earn money but also spends time with his family may think they are just doing their job to make a few dollars. However, spending time with his family shows how important family is to him.

Family relationships are important to him. is an aspect of who he is. This makes him feel that his existence isn't void of meaning. In fact, within his family, he understands the larger significance of life.

Furthermore faith in the notion of the real self affects the way that people treat people who suffer from mental illness. For instance, the students who are willing to take medication for ADHD is because certain people believe that concentration is to be a major element of their identity. This medication allows students to concentrate on their classes. However people with bipolar disorder don't want to take their medication as they fear that the medications could alter the characteristics and traits of their actual personas.

How do you become your authentic self and accept your true self?

Being your authentic self means you don't search for happiness anyplace. If you're being the person you are and you aren't afraid or avoid pain. You don't need people's approval or admiration. You don't scream at other people, or think about taking on someone else to get fame or power. You are respectful of the other human beings as they are naturally genuine and authentic. You don't want to see any living being suffering, nor would you wish to be an individual's cause. You are a lover of yourself and the people who surround you. You try to understand other people's issues and the reasons why people behave in a certain manner. You accept people's mistakes, and you forgive yourself too. You aren't denying that you've wronged yourself. Instead, you acknowledge it as a public statement. This is what your authentic self.

Many people aren't comfortable with their true nature or are scared to admit their true self. This can be due to a variety of reasons.

* You believe in the other's head:

If you are constantly thinking about the people around you are going to say about you or say about you to other people that you are not the person you are. You are trapped in the bubble which prevents you from doing what you want to do. You constantly judge yourself at every turn. You are exhausted and you lose your energy, time and energy trying to accomplish things that will be pleasing or impress others while not doing things that you enjoy and love. You show only a tiny part of yourself in the way you perceive it in comparison to other people's views and where people aren't likely to criticize your actions.

* The comparison can make things more difficult:

If you are constantly comparing yourself and your life to other people, you cease to be the person you are. You are pushed off an unintentional path that leads you after things others have , but not you. It causes you to feel like you're not yourself during this trip. Your focus is on how to look similar to others or be more successful than the others.

Your child scored an A+ and the neighbor's child scored an A. However, your child is involved in hobbies like sports and the arts which the other child doesn't. If you force your child to not participate in other extra-curricular activities and force him to concentrate on his studies then you'll see your child lose his real self, as he is a person who is a fan of games and engage in arts.

* Listening to others too often:

If you listen to other's advice and suggestions too often, you lose the ability to choose which actions to take and what to avoid doing. Every step of your journey you are dependent on people's approval and approval. You cease to believe in your own decisions and beliefs. Even if a suggestion from someone else isn't asked for listening to others' opinions could lead you to believe in things that aren't actually true even if they are true. When you begin believing the lies that people continue to recite in your mind, you start to conceal your true self within and you make decisions as per what people tell you. You begin to believe that you must be happy for others and not be yourself. This can be a challenge since you're no longer the real you.

* When you're struggling, you get angry:

If you are faced with difficult times one after the another, you stop being positive and interpreting things from a positive perspective. You are frustrated, and not being able to show who you truly are. You begin to see things in the wrong direction and you don't pay attention to the truth of who you are.

The above mentioned are just a few reasons people find it difficult to accept themselves as they are.

What happens if you stop the truth about yourself?

When you find yourself incapable of accepting your true self, you will lose several things: joy, contentment and self-esteem. confidence in yourself, and so on. You lose the ability to think and make choices independently. You feel less content in trying to make others content. You lose your satisfaction when you are unable to make people feel satisfied by your actions.

Your self-awareness disappears. When you're no longer committed to your self, it affects the ability to be authentic and honest with others around you. It affects your relationships, friends, family as well as colleagues. Additionally, you are more susceptible to mental disorders like anxiety, depression and stress.

Chapter 7: Body Language And attitude

In the coming days or so, I would like you to watch the people around you. It could be sitting in a cafe , and taking note of the people around you. Notepads are handy because I want you to understand that confidence does not have anything to do with appearance or size, or anything of such a nature. Look around and see which individuals are confident. These are people who don't hesitate to talk to strangers and display the following body language

The heads of the people walking with them are elevated

* They smile

* They can converse with others

* They don't make mistakes.

Try to identify people who may be suffering from self-esteem issues or have a lack of confidence. The way they express themselves will be different

* They are reluctant to communicate.

* They have their heads lowered or without even looking at the people in front of them.

* They could fumble

* They might not be certain of their position

There are many aspects that can help you make it clear to the world that are confident, however there are also body language signals that inform others in your vicinity that you're experiencing issues. Be aware of what these signals are, as you might be shocked to realize that you are displaying numerous body language signs.

Then, place a complete length mirror in a spot that can be observed from the entryway in your room. Step out, close the door. Then, let it open, and observe your entry. Take a look at how you position your body. Take a look at the posture on your neck. Are your shoulders relaxed? Do you cross your arms? Do you look confident? I'd be willing to bet that you'll make the same mistakes that individuals make, but these are fairly easy to fix when you understand the reasons behind them. The way you sit and how you stand, as well as the way you interact with others are all indicators. With that information take a walk outside once more and try to improve your posture so that you only convey positive signals. Do you notice the change? You might also want to consider your style of dressing. If you're constantly changing your clothes, then you're likely to be uncomfortable wearing them. Perhaps you should seek out styles that will help you feel good. If you've got clothes you've got in the closet but do not make you feel good it could be the perfect time to eliminate the items.

The issue that a lot of people face is that they save their clothes hoping that they'll be able to be able to fit again, but each time you look at them, you are reminded of the mistakes you made. This is not a good idea. Make sure you have things that help you feel happy. If you're an individual who suffers from depression Do you dress in many dark colors? It's time to lighten your mood slightly. What about that pot stomach? Do you try to cover it beneath layers of clothes? Try something more snug even if it's the size you normally don't wear? The purpose for this activity is to cause you to feel confident about how you look. If you're thought to be insecure about yourself, consider the shoes you are wearing. Are you able to walk confidently wearing them or are they restricting your movements? This isn't about style. It's about feeling comfortable in an area that is public.

For you to feel confident in yourself To feel self-esteem, you must feel confident about yourself. we'll get to this in the following chapter. For now, however think about the way you walk into a room and attempt to model your behavior by the confident people you saw in others in the vicinity. Actually, try to imagine whom among your friends is confident . Then, make your entrance a model for the person you think is confident. It's possible but you have to keep at it until eventually, you're the one that you're playing. If you are struggling with self-esteem that show up in the public because your subconscious is aware of entering a space with strangers or sitting next to someone and speaking. You must re-record your thoughts, so you can make an effort to confront the world with a straight face today, and pay attention to your body expressions. Also, you need to be comfortable speaking to others, and I've given you some additional tasks to complete this week.

Exercises to build confidence and self-esteem

I'd like you to talk to an individual who isn't yours and ask them what the time is. It's not difficult to do, however I would like you to look them in the eye , and after they've told you the time, you should acknowledge them and then walk away. These are people who are not your friends. What you're doing is reducing the fear of strangers through regularly making contact with strangers you do not have a relationship with. The other thing you can talk about is weather. If you are in a car with someone, you can talk about the good or bad your weather has been. You must come out of the shell you've been hiding behind as well. The more often you accomplish this the more positive the message that is forming in your brain. It will become easier and easier to do so. becomes more easy and less difficult with the practice.

The second thing I want you to complete this week is enter an area that is crowded and keep your head up high. It could be any type of gathering. Take a look around you, and decide on whom you want to discuss with. Choose your way of approaching. Make a list of what you planning to say and limit yourself the conversation to a small scale. If you are lacking of confidence in yourself, you do not want to be involved in arguments or say something that you're not comfortable with. So, just show your true self and tell someone else to do something that doesn't have any significance. Maybe you could introduce yourself or ask for a place to have a drink.

Chapter 8: intolerance Faced By

Women In Work Area

In our discussion, we discussed the process of achieving self-love and the ways we can tackle it to get greater levels of self-love in our life.

Be kind to yourself and accept yourself.

In our everyday lives we do not have control over what is happening that surround us. For instance, we can't alter the behavior and attitudes of people around us. We can't alter our appearance i.e. the color of our eyes and skin hairstyle, color, body language, etc. The only thing we control is our perception of our self. Consider all the negative actions or incidents that you've encountered from others with some salt. It's not about blind acceptance of boundaries but accepting that you aren't able to change the behavior of people or events from the past could go a long way toward healing.

Be grateful

After having a rough past, you're now right today. Be thankful for being shown the lessons you need to master and If you are willing to do the required effort to improve yourself, then you'll be rewarded for taking on your own personal "dark knight'.

Keep your optimism your mind focused on the fact that the entirety of your day, and in fact, the rest of your life is in the future and your most memorable years are to be! Don't worry about the little things. Sometimes, our worst nightmares be, in the end, turn out to be our greatest gifts. If you are able to change the way you think about things and the things you think about can change.

Also, remember that every person is fighting their own battles in this world. This isn't to say you must accept whatever you're confronted with however, having the awareness that a lot of us struggle too can aid in understanding why certain people behave in as they do.

The treatment of depression

Depression is the biggest threat to self-esteem. It's a condition that affects your confidence even when good circumstances are occurring to you. Therefore, you should be conscious of the times when depression takes over since this issue can cause you to lose confidence in yourself as you begin to make negative comments about yourself.

Find out the root of the depression and pinpoint the root of the issue. This is one of the most beneficial ways you can to increase your level of self-love. Many people do not bother to do this, that results in the absence of healing injuries.

There are bad things that can happen to all people in everyday life. Therefore, be aware of your thoughts and if you find yourself sinking to a world of despair, change your attitude, perhaps taking a stroll in the park or an exercise class. It's easy to fall into depression if you don't feel confident in yourself, and being conscious of this is the first step in safeguarding yourself. Do whatever you can to conquer these obstacles.

Dissolve conflicts or establish healthy boundaries

Sometimes, we face difficult decisions to make. Our loved ones and close friends, or even coworkers can test our patience to the limit. There are many people who are hurt and have a desire to hurt other people. Understanding when to forgive or establish healthy boundaries is crucial. There is a widespread belief that because someone is a family member or blood related that you must always return to the empty bowl just like dogs. You are entitled to leave anyone you encounter who is not up to the boundaries.

Sometimes, we stay several years or even longer than we ought to in toxic and unhealthy relationships, which cause more damage over the long term.

Sometimes, we become accustomed to being treated as dirt that it can become the same cycle seems to be impossible to break.

The positive side is that you are able to escape and continue on the road of building self-esteem, hanging out with the energy vampires will not be able help you get where you want to be!

There's no harm in forgiveness however, only if you are at a point where you are confident and ready. Have they apologized? Are they feeling remorseful? Healthy boundaries are essential for self-love. It's not easy initially but you'll feel grateful that you put them in and you'll probably be wondering why you didn't act sooner!

However If you decide to forgive someone, take it on faith. There's no reason to keep raising issues from the past repeating the same thing if you've already decided to let go and go on.

Always remember that balance is the most important thing healthy boundaries are at the top of the list when discussing a healthy self-esteem.

History

While many consider confidence and self-esteem as being closely linked however, there are many aspects that distinguish them. When you look at these comparisons, consider the parts of your lives you might be having difficulty in. Keep a note of situations that are like ones you've experienced. These will be used later in this chapter, to assist you to increase your self-awareness.

Self-Confidence is Situational

One of the main distinctions between self-confidence and self-esteem is how they display. A person with a high self-esteem generally feels comfortable about themselves regardless of circumstances. If they are satisfied with their job and are generally satisfied about the job they perform in their home and beyond the workplace. Confidence in oneself, however is subject to change depending upon the circumstance. A person could be extremely confident about their abilities to manage or work as part of the team, but have a lack of confidence in crunching numbers or engaging in sports. You can feel confident in one aspect of life , but not feel confident in the other. It is because self-confidence is domain-specific and self-esteem covers every aspect of our lives.

One obvious example is retired tennis pro Andre Agassi, who is widely regarded as one of the best tennis players of the past. It is evident the fact that Agassi is confident about his skills as a player despite claims later that his dislike of tennis was a result of his childhood. Although Agassi was a tennis pro but he was lacking self-esteem and a general sense of self-confidence in other areas in his personal life. Recently, he's revealed his experience with anxiety, depression, and addiction to drugs which has shown that even those who appear competent or successful in their chosen journey may struggle with low self-esteem.

Building Self-Confidence. Building Self-Esteem

In general, it's more straightforward to build confidence in yourself than self-esteem. Self-confidence is built by doing something or becoming proficient at doing something. As people progress across their journeys, they've made accomplishments and their lists of talents and accomplishments increase. While these accomplishments can boost self-confidence but they don't increase self-love. Self-esteem can't be achieved by constructing an arsenal of abilities in the event that those skills do not enhance a person's perception of them.

Factors that affect self-esteem

Self-esteem grows as time passes. As a young person self-esteem means that you are content externally. Friends at school and siblings, parents and any other family members you are close to play a significant part in your feelings about yourself. If they provide positive feedback, it can help increase confidence in yourself. In the same way, how they treat you can affect the way you view your role in the world.

One reason individuals struggle with self-esteem is the fact that they didn't receive the affirmation and encouragement that they needed to realize their worth within the society. People with low self-esteem remain in a state of struggle when they become teenagers. Even if they get praise from peers, they may be unable to handle the judgement or criticism of their parents. There are many other things that impact self-esteem when you're an adult. This includes:

• Your impression of the other.

* How others perceive you

* The way you see other people

* Work experience or at school

* The presence of illness or disability

* Traditions of religion or culture

In these various aspects those that you control the most on are the thoughts and standing. It's likely that most of the methods offered to boost self-esteem concentrate on changing your mindset and how you view things around you. This allows for change to occur from within.

Discourse on the discrimination that women face

Affirmative action is a collection of guidelines and actions created to end the discrimination that has been in place for a long time in the context of race or color, sex, national origin. However, in modern times discrimination is typically regarded as undesirable.

The Case Study shall discuss unfavorable discrimination based on Nigerian customary law on inheritance, especially in relation to women widows, widows, and the girl child, which is a source of discrimination based on sexual orientation, and also as it affects people who are not legitimate that are discriminated against in relation to the circumstances surrounding a person's birth.

Discrimination based on customary inheritance rules, especially in relation to women and those who are not legitimate is a very actual and ongoing problem within various Nigerian communities, even despite the recent changes in the law that are supposed to change the issue, or change or alter the practices.

However, discrimination isn't restricted to Nigeria it is a worldwide phenomenon that is a reality even in civilized nations of the world like the United States of America, India, South African, etc. For instance, in the United States for instance, discrimination based on the principle of being separate but equal that was applied to people due to race or color was in place during the period of forty-six years from 1896 when it received an approval from the judiciary from the United States Supreme Court in the case of Plessy v. Ferguson and 1954 when the United States Supreme Court overruled itself in the case of Brown v. Board of Education. In India there were long periods of discrimination due to the caste system was in existence that saw those in the bottom of the castes, referred to as untouchables, were subject to discrimination as poor and were the target of oppression, violence and exclusion. Also in South Africa there was also many years of discrimination imposed by the Apartheid South African government as an official policy that was based on gender and race. These discriminatory practices are being swept away thanks to the affirmative action policies implemented by the governments of both these governments to end the discriminatory policies.

It is believed that the Nigerian alternative to affirmative action refers to the federal rule that was incorporated into different sections of the constitution in 1999. However, none of this principle addressed the issue with discrimination in the treatment of women unlegitimate individuals and various other groups.

In the instance of the Sokwo case. Kpongbo the Nigerian Supreme Court reiterated this decision as follows:

It is a well-established principle to the law that customary laws are a matter of fact that must be proven through evidence. The burden is on the party who asserts that there is a specific custom. He has to present evidence that is credible to prove its existence. However, it is also clear that when an existing custom has been adequately determined by the court it is possible to issue a judicial notice that the same may be taken and the court does not need further evidence of the identical custom.

If law truly is an instrument for social engineering as well as an instrument of growth, as repeated by jurists and scholars and other scholars, then the approach of the judiciary should be to utilize the instrument of the law to adapt to the changing social and economic conditions. But, as a blessing, as will be demonstrated in this study the provisions in the 1999 constitution, the recent court decisions, as well as the international human rights instruments have all risen to the occasion. It will be revealed through the Study that the present state of Nigerian law has enacted a ban on the unfair customary inheritance rules. What is required in the present moment is not just a codification or reformation of the existing traditions, which suggested by certain quarters and others, but in order to close the gap in place between the present situation of Nigerian legal system and customs of the different Nigerian communities.

Chapter 9: result Of Low Self-Esteem

On Your societal Life

Self-esteem issues can affect how you socialize, among other issues. Because of this, many people with low self-esteem are likely to take initiatives to avoid social situations, whichultimatelymay lead to an increase in self-esteem.

Since of Low Self-Esteem, Avoidance of a Social Life

This could also be a sign of anxiety and social stress that can be entangled with low self-esteem. If you experience intense feelings of fear and anxiety, it may lower the self-esteem you have. Social anxiety and low self-esteem can enhance one the other.

Unfortunately, evasion isn't a healthy or well-balanced method of dealing with the anxiety of social interaction or a low self-esteem. If you've planned to go out, but anxiety about mingling with others or self-criticism start to creep into your life, it could be helpful to repeat the following expression yourself within your head: "Feel the worry and also do it anyhow."

Anxiety could be a challenge for you, but it only disrupts your life when you live in response to it. Accepting your anxiety and stress or self-criticism as it is requires a lot of endurance. The ability to perform this is among the most efficient ways to build self-confidence.

Low Self-Esteem, as well as Social interactions- Self-Criticism

If you're someone who struggles with low self-esteem when socializing with others, you may experience irritated self-criticism, both during and following the social interaction. If you're living with low self-esteem, it's easy to convince yourself yourself of the reasons that others might not like you , since it's easy to feel self-conscious about yourself.

It is essential to inform on your own and ensure that nobody is evaluating your work as you do. Everyone is as concerned than you.

Low Self-Esteem and Not Speaking About Your Social Life

It is possible to keep a tight protection of your thoughts and feelings in social situations when you feel self-esteem is low. The risk of being ridiculed or rejected could be thought of the same and hinder you from speaking up and sharing your thoughts. It is also possible to create the impression that you don't have anything worth mentioning and that no one wants to hear what you have to say when you feel less self-esteem within your social circle.

Being shy due to a lack of self-esteem your social circle can cause you to lose the opportunity to make a lot of friends particularly in relation to your the job you have and your relationships. Another thing to consider is the expression: "really feel the worry and also do it anyhow," will help in this regard. It assists you in establishing the self-image of a balanced and healthy person that allows you to engage in social settings with confidence.

Impact of Low Self-Esteem on Your Relationships

When you're facing a difficult separation or losing the task at hand, everyone struggles with low self-esteem from time to time. If something goes wrong is normal for your inner movie critic to scream and declare things like, "You're unsatisfactory," or "You'll never ever more than happy."

It's normal to have varying self-esteem, particularly when life throws your way with a flurry of events, when your self-esteem is constantly lacking any, it may be a negative influence, not only on you but also on your wonderful acquaintances.

Are you struggling with low self-esteem? It's not uncommon to experience difficulty dealing with a low self-image and you may find that you're feeling a sense of uncertainty or doubt as well as anxiety. In addition, if you are constantly stung by these negative ideas and feelings about the self-esteem you have built up in your self-esteem, they could influence your relationship with your partner in a variety of ways.

The Science of How Low Self-Esteem Impacts Relationships

The study reveals that self-esteem could affect your happiness in the relationship regardless of how it impacts the relationship of your partner. If you're unhappy about yourself the instabilities you feel can start to creep into the way you present yourself to your spouse-- which could have a negative effect on both of you.

A low self-esteem may alter the perception you have of your partner According to research studies by the

Journal of Personality and also Social Psychology. In the study, researchers asked more than 500 females and males to complete sets of questions about their self-esteem. They then inquired about how scared they were by the problems of their friends. The people with low self-esteem were not only more frightened by their partner's imperfections, but they also were more likely to interpret their relationship in black-and-white terms, namely as all good or all poor.

Being able to have that kind of unbalanced view of your spouse could be a challenge for your relationship, says Steven Graham, PhD, researcher in charge of the study and associate professor in psychology in the New College of Florida in Sarasota. "If my sights of you are transforming really promptly, believing extremely favorably regarding you one min and also adversely the following, that might make the various other individual really feel unconfident," Graham says.

In a relationship, predictability is crucial, says. It's been proven to be an important indicator of the quality of the love between a couple.

As well as affecting your perception of your partner, having low self-esteem may also cause you to feel more anxious about your relationship in general. "You might hesitate that your companion will certainly leave you, or you worry over various other points that would not hesitate about," states Heidi Riggio, PhD, psychotherapist for social issues and also an aide to a psychology teacher of California State University in Los Angeles. "This can cause anxiety attack or severe envy."

If your self-esteem has fallen into the dirt, it will be with you for the rest of your life, regardless of where you are. This is the same for our relationships. If self-respect is lacking at a minimum the connection with you will fall down with it.

The baggage you carry is bound to follow you into your relationship. In the Journal of Personality and also Social Psychology located that individuals with low self-esteem ended up feeling worried about their partner's rent-related blemishes. "If my sights of you are altering really swiftly, believing extremely favorably concerning you one min as well as adversely the following, that might make the various other individual really feel troubled," explained Steven Graham, Ph.D. who was the principal author of the study.

This is how self-esteem issues can cause further problems in your relationships.

There is a problem connecting.

All of us require balanced and healthy interactions to keep our relationships running. The ability to communicate your emotions is essential for a successful and increasing relationship. A relationship can't be established without interaction.

You become poisonous.

134

There is a problem in the event that you're showing signs that you are putting someone down regularly.

You must discover why you're using like this and is threatening your relationship. These issues have been driving your actions, Psychology Today shared. You can ask yourself whether you are the one who causes harm and be honest about the issue.

It's easy to become self-important.

If you depend on your partner to provide an ongoing psychological support and a constant focus on them, it could be affecting the relationship. What happens is that you'll be able to sense the tension in the event that your happiness is contingent on a single person. Don't ever expect your loved one to meet all of your needs socially and have every emotion you feel with them because it's not healthy and balanced.

You can choose to fight.

We know that all connections have them! You know in your heart that if direct encounter with a conflict can make you feel uncomfortable, and you need to rebuild your self-esteem. If there are problems it is important to address them, not hide from them.

You are constantly slapped by the person on a regular basis.

If we're feeling anxious and also suffer from a lack of self-esteem, we'll often feel as if the other person is threatening us. However, even if what they're saying may not be true those who are sure of themselves will not let their self-esteem to suffer. "Although joy normally decreases somewhat over time, this isn't real for individuals that get in a partnership with greater degrees of self-esteem," the licensed marital relationship and as and family members expert Darlene Lancer outlined.

You are in control.

If a person believes that they are not worthy of the value to their personal viewpoint and themselves, it can turn out to be more difficult for them to keep relationships. It is essential that people within a group have their own space to breathe. If they don't it, they'll become angry and could even begin withdrawing from the relationship.

You End up Settling for Less Than You Deserve

In many cases, those with issues with self-esteem are prone to having a relationship break up because they believe that they're not entitled to any kind of superior treatment. A lot of people stay with a person who might be unkind to them and/or does provide them with care generous, compassion, and psychological aid because they don't believe that they're worthy. Being in a stale and unfulfilling relationship with someone who does not appreciate you will make you feel worse later on.

Your Connection Stays on a Superficial Level

Additionally there are many people who aren't totally devoted to their loved ones due to uncertainty. Simply put due to an insufficient self-image, it could be that you think that being honest, open and also sincere could make your partner feel uncomfortable. If you're cautious and are hesitant to share your truth and be the real you and be yourself, you'll never get to understand your friend at a more deep and more intimate level because you're not being the authentic you.

You Have Negative Expectations About Your Relationship

Another way that low self-esteem could damage your connection to your partner is when it causes you to develop a negative perception of the relationship the relationship itself. In addition, if you believe that you don't need to have a happy, healthy and healthy, and long-lasting relationship, it could directly affect your future actions and actions and end up as a self-fulfilling predication. Particularly, if you think that your relationship is likely to fail by a certain amount, you're actually creating the foundation for that result to take place.

You act in a clingy and Clingy way

In the majority of instances those who have low self-esteem tend to become dependent, jealous and even controlled. Because due to a lack or self-esteem may find yourself wanting to spend all day with your partner because you are constantly worried about whether or not he/she is going to be a sour note to you. If you change into someone who acts in a way that is clingy however, the reality is that this behavior will make your partner more hesitant to be with you.

You Constantly Need Reassurance

Furthermore, having less self-esteem could affect your relationship with your partner by causing you constantly seek confidence in him or her. Because due to your instability you could find on your own constantly asking your partner if he is still interested in you or whether you're really cute. This type of question will make it difficult for them and also to convince you to believe that you're good enough and they could make your friend look into their real feelings for you.

Bring the Bling

Maybe he did repeatedly, and your relationship is bound made you feel like this once again. It is possible that you feel pressured to limit yourself to your ideals of excellence as the standard you set for your beautiful friends to be up to. Even if your partner turns into someone who is steady, dependable and compassionate, you may be able to invalidate your efforts and discover ways to weaken the bond.

Testing

It is hard to imagine that you're really enjoying yourself and therefore you scrutinize your companion at every opportunity that you get to ensure they can demonstrate their worth (which you don't think or trust in any way). You could also ruin your relationship due to the reality that you know your partner will leave at any time. At the end of every connection, it lets you claim, "See, I informed you of this.

Protected

If your dads and moms had a difficult breakup or a relationship that was shattered and you are feeling insecure about your partner now, regardless of whether you are aware of your security or not. You could be worried and hesitant of allowing yourself to wish to abandon your friend before you are abandoned or allow yourself to be completely entangled in an alliance from the beginning. If you are relying on the possibility that you will not be deceived You are genuinely scared of exposing yourself to the risk of being hurt.

Resistant

Birthed, which means that they have to do the it is a difficult task to gain the capacity, regardless of adverse experiencesto be a part of an effective, positive relationship as they grow. Maybe there was a few at some point in her life who provided advice and help and helped her in overcoming her low self-esteem through endurance.

You're with your partner for the wrong reasons

Furthermore, people who lack self-esteem are often in connection for uninformed motivations. They may also be scared of being on their own or worried about what other people might think should they break up their relationship. If you're worried about opinions of other people and are also afraid of being viewed as a failure and in danger of failing your partner and yourself by staying in a relationship due to all the wrong factors.

Boy-Crazy

When you're feeling low self-esteem it may appear like nothing is happening promptly or in a normal way to you. If the connection doesn't develop quickly or according to your schedule, it can be difficult to bear. This is a signal to work more.

Looking For Financial Safety

Are you ready to give up your expectations for a true relationship with a person that will provide you with a broad range of options as well as economic safety and security? It also provides the mental security of control: you are in charge of your capacity to please men without having to give away your heart.

Looking for Insecurity

Because you're familiar with circumstances that lower self-esteemsuch as being abandoned in the dark, getting ripped off by the other hand, etc.you're drawn to relationships that allow you to experience this familiar insecurity. You're used to working to maintain a shaky relationship that these types of relationships tend to be the only ones that you are drawn toward.

Settlers

You're ready to commit on yourself to an one who shares your passion. You'll be more tolerant of the person the person you choose. You may also wish to accept a lifestyle that don't please you because you feel blessed to be with someone however you are aware that you're not happy.

Terrified of Intimacy

You could be very scared when the relationship progresses because a authentic link feels fake and also so global. Instead of allowing the link to work, it may be able to retrace your steps and be a bit less distant psychologically as well as sexually distant.

Shock

In order to secure your self that you are not deceiving yourself, you also think of deceiving from a simple companion that in turn, sours the relationship as time goes along. When you doubt your partner often, perhaps frequently that he might begin to consider making the right choice. He is "doing the time" so why would he not commit the criminal charge?

A balanced and healthy connection includes value, purpose and precepts that are based on and a sense of oneness. Self-esteem may be positive pressure in a relationship or cause harm to it.

We are all aware of numerous other ways that women show lower self-esteem in relationships. The ability to recognize yourself will help guide you away from these patterns of low self-esteem within relationships to appreciate, understanding and incorporating your thoughts, actions, and ideas.

Chapter 10: Bring Positive

Affirmations For Change Your Life

A positive mindset is the best way to be content and living a happy life. Our thoughts do an immense role in the how we feel. Moreover, the act of thinking constructively can keep an person to be positive throughout the day but pessimism can lead to low confidence , and you are able to pass through a large amount of your time. We often get ourselves into a rut and do not even realize we're doing it in this way. Whenever negative thoughts are floating around our minds. We put our feet on something that is over the top and sow seeds of doubt. There's a small but effective tool that you can employ

throughout the day to alter the negative thoughts and instill an ever-positive outlook; using positive affirmations every day will improve your life.

Certain. They will make you more certain, more mindful and more sure about yourself. They can also help you see yourself to a wider range of viewpoints to enhance your life.

What are affirmations that can be positive?

The positive affirmations that you can use are used throughout the day , wherever and anytime you require them. the more you utilize them, the more positive thoughts can take over negative ones , and you'll be able to see positive effects within your daily life. A statement is a fundamental method that can be used to overcome negative self-talk is often not even conscious of.

doing, to engaging in a look at your life by progressively improving your attitude. Most of us have long been apathetic about our lives, and this is why you should change your concerns and the ways you imagine will not happen, but in the event that you continue to use certifications, they'll be useful once you've changed your outlook. There is a variety of methods for coping with diverse situations that arise in your daily life. The most common and efficient are listed below.

The mirror technique

This approach helps you be yourself and to build awareness and confidence. You should be in front of an mirror, at least an entire length mirror just your clothes, or perhaps stripped. Start with your head, and work your way down your body. tell everyone what you enjoy about certain areas of your body such as you can declare "I like the manner in which my hair sparkles, the slight contrasts in shading where the light hits it" or " my eyes are gorgeous shades of __. They sparkle and shine My eyes are a fantastic part of my body" Take your time and take a step by step approach to the whole of your body, creating an ever-positive image of yourself.

The technique of relocating

This method can be used at any time and anywhere you begin to think of about negative thoughts If you realize that you're thinking of an unfavourable thought, consider taking a handle off of a volume inside your head , with the aim of turning the volume down to a level so that you do not be able to hear it. When you are done, think of you can find a positive affirmation to counter the negative, and then raise the volume repeating it to yourself.

The technique of the trash can

In the event that you are contemplating negative thoughts, write your thoughts on a sheet paper, roll the paper into a ball and throw it in the trash bin and by doing so, you're telling yourself those thoughts are merely waste , and that's the only place where they can find a space.

The technique of meditation

Find a quiet spot in which you can unwind for 5 or 10 minutes. shut your eyes and let your mind go to sleep. all things being equal and your emotions. Begin to repeat your affirmation to your self over and over again, as you focus on the words that you are repeating, and be sure to believe what you're saying.

Chapter 11: Self-Discipline and Inertia

"So many fail due to the fact that they

They don't want to get started. They don't

move. They can't conquer.

Inertia. They don't start."

-Ben Stein

Biologically, we are aware that all of us acquire knowledge through instruction, communication and facts. As society presents an image of a bright prosperous, wealthy, successful and wealthy but the image projected by society upon the exhausted is not reality. It's a figment of imagination.

However how powerful your brain can guide your life. Instead of being guided by feelings that are erratic and unpredictable, everyone ought to listen to their more intelligent thinking. This is the tough part one has to learn how to transcend certain limitations of the body by utilizing an inertial principle.

The law of inertia says that movement or direction is not resisted. When applied to human beings every person feels that resistance whenever the alarm goes off at dawn. In reality there is more to it than just moan! When you're in a state of in a state of relaxation, there is a strong desire to still. This is known as inertia.

Also, you might not be able to make a written report for work or at home. You don't feel like searching for a word in the dictionary; you'd prefer to grab a quick food rather than prepare your own meal. You might avoid for grocery shopping until your fridge has nothing other than a dead banana.

Emotions and thoughts are often interchangeable. It happens when the mighty power of the mind responds to the demands of the emotional centers. Instead of restraining the thoughts and activities of one's mind to improve self-esteem and progress in life, emotions can come up and hinder the process of reaching your maximum potential. If emotions are allowed to dictate their thinking, they will allow their fundamental urges to rule them.

The desire to be at peace (inertia)

The need for relaxation

The desire for enjoyable interactions with friends via the internet (rather than working)

The desire to have food

Involvement in sexual activities in situations that are inappropriate

Procrastination

Work performance that is not as enthusiastic

The emotions of people can be used as a reason for inability to discipline behaviour. If someone is experiencing anxiety and anxious, they may decide to decide to take the rest of the day off instead of addressing their fear and accept the fact that it exists, and continue to move on. If someone is depressed depression may become an easy routine. Instead of going out and socialize with friends one might choose to stay at home lying in sleeping. Arguments similar to those that were discussed in the preceding chapter could flood your mind. For instance, someone could say "I'll never see anyone there. The guys will all ignore me. I'm a slob. This pimple isn't removed."

Your mind's rationality is a powerful tool. Utilize and strengthen your thinking to boost your energy. Pay attention to every thought you make. Be positive with yourself. If you aren't happy with an idea you've just thought of be aware of it. Find a new perspective which will provide you with an optimistic view of the subject you thought about.

In 1995, psychologist Daniel Goleman, coined the term "Emotional IQ," meaning that people are able to control their emotions using their brain's higher center known as the neo-cortex. If you activate the higher brain areas you can categorize your emotions and modify your behavior in that your actions reflect the mood of your brain, not your emotions. It is possible to smile. Simply smiling can release the biochemical known as gaba which produces a pleasant sensation stimulating relaxation in which the environment is ideal for rational thought. Gaba can also reduce stress and anxiety. It is often referred to as "nature's valium."

Chapter 12: How to Building Mental Toughness

We are not made mentally strong or weak. We are growing into tiny beings who are capable of overcoming, improving and building. Chess plays a crucial role in this process of maturation.

How do you define mental power? A state of mind that is peaceful and courage, we could describe it as a relationship to the world which allows the advancement of one's life. A sufficient amount of resilience to stand quickly following a accident. The more powerful our minds are is, the more easily we are capable of resolving our anxiety-related and negative thinking.

The question is, how can we be mentally strong or is it a natural condition? If the environment and training are crucial to our perception of the world taking the time to understand them will allow us to gain mental strength slowly.

The autumn

To achieve this, we need to be able to fall and to rise, and learn to accept the fall, without failing. The difference between a fall and failure is that in the former instance, a fall is an act, and has an end and a beginning in contrast to failure, which is a form of closure.

If you include into your thinking that failure is not a thing as such, and make use of it to discover ways improve and to get up to restart, you'll understand that you can't achieve success unless we suffer through a series of falls that give us a clue that is to rise up and keep going. This is why the one who starts a business that is ultimately unsuccessful and then is yet again denied to the countless applications submitted for months but isn't able to switch work, or the person that fails to achieve its goals or goals, the one constantly confronted by an angry and obnoxious boss, has to learn to experience the negative feeling in order to learn how to do things differently. This is where the psychological force starts,

Learning

The fall is the beginning of learning. Learn how to get up, think in a solution-oriented manner. Being able to adjust to situations of crisis requires knowledge of the complexities of crisis. We don't know, we just want to view the issue "in theory," and it isn't the complete reflection of the reality. It is essential to conduct all learning, and to be aware of what you are learning. If, for instance, you are, month upon month, confronted by an authority structure which claims you are the one responsible for information which concern you, there are a variety of options. Continue to endure and hope for an improvement on the outside. The hierarchy may change For example. This is a risky option. In reality, there is nothing that depends on you. This means that you are essentially passive when it comes to the situation.

The other option is to understand it, The "why" and the "how." Who is this hierarchy composed of? Why do they delegate their duties? What can I do to safeguard myself? What should I do to protect myself? If you're trying to comprehend that you are at the forefront of learning. Follow your strengths analysis that leads you to implement strategies to get the best position. Don't let your feelings get in the way and place you in a state of helplessness.

The information

Through falling and learning comes the ability to learn. The more you are aware of things and the more likely it is not afraid. Fear of failing is a fear that comes with trying something new, fear of making changes the worry about losing your entire life... The list goes on. of these fears are rooted in looking at the world that makes you immobile. The basis of knowledge is mental strength. Mental power allows you to think regardless of whether the earth shakes.

What do we really mean by knowing? In addition to your daily lifelong learning, learn the most possible about the direction you're headed. From general knowledge to anecdotal wisdom. This one can help you in the next. In particular when you are in the presence of your manager who wants to let you go, stating that he'll recommend you, for instance it is best to be fully understanding of your rights, interests and desires. Three areas of knowledge to share and keep. Also, if you're involved in the event of an employee being wrongly targeted be sure to judge yourself against someone you've dismissed. If you're satisfied with the information of the lawyers, your bosses and friends' examples You become fragile. Your words are a reflection of inexperience. Each situation is a challenge that requires the necessary knowledge. The knowledge gained in the midst of a crises is part of the internal tools you'll need to use in any conflict.

How do we develop mental toughness?

Consider the mental force to be the muscle.

As with athletes who train to build physical strength and mental strength, mental strength is an muscle that requires continuous stimulation. Do you think that a bodybuilder is able to be successful in a competition if he is not working his muscles daily? The same is true for your mind. The most successful people who exist or have been around for a while possess a unshakeable mental power. This power allows them to withstand the tests. They knew that without a strong mentality there is no way to succeed over the long haul.

Enjoy a pleasant living space

A positive environment is among the primary factors that determine success.

We view our own self through the eyes of other people. A smile that is kind could inspire confidence even when a malicious and accusatory stare could keep you from any motive.

Pediatrician Catherine Gueguen tells us that: "any harmonious interaction, a warm atmosphere, a pleasant conversation, a shared pleasure provoke the secretion of oxytocin." So being in a healthy environment that has harmonious relationships will let the release of the hormone responsible for happiness and wellbeing. Hormone essential to develop mental strength.

The process of getting to know each other

To handle doubts and criticism that is not substantiated To deal with doubts and criticism, it is essential to be aware of each other. This means knowing one's strengths, but also weaknesses. People who succeed aren't those who have no weaknesses, but instead those who understood these weaknesses to be able to overcome them.

It is typical for those who don't have a relationship to quit easily since they don't know the motivations behind them. Many people are unaware of what their life's purpose is and find themselves around in circles. We're losing many years of living in a void due to the inability to recognize the self.

Retake control

The lack of control over your life can leave us with an uncomfortable state. The majority of people surrender their authority to others, such as their familymembers, their boss, spouses, friends or even politicians. We let others make our decisions for us.

For a mind that can last forever it is necessary to regain control over your life. Deciding who you are, or what you'd like to be, could make a some difference. To control your life and increase your mental power You must take control of your life . You must choose what is right for you. Do not let other people dictate who you are or what you want your life to be about.

Chess is a game that can be used to create opportunities.

Chess is only played by those not strong enough in their minds. People who are successful are optimistic and see chess as an opportunity to improve their skills. The people who have succeeded in achieving their goals have walked many obstacles. It is rare for people to reach their goal without enduring one or more infamous mistakes. The issue isn't a failure, but rather our response to failure. Therefore, for people who have a solid mind the word "failure" is not a thing by itself!

Accept the challenges

If you're a person with enough mental power, the challenges and mistakes, shouldn't worry you. It's not easy to achieve the goal you want and trust it until the final. One of the most important factors that make up mental power is courage. It is essential to face challenges with courage and never doubt yourself or the value of your plan. The mental strength you have will enable you to over adversity.

Being clear of oneself.

One of the major causes of failure lies in the reality that people aren't confident about their abilities. Before you begin a project, you must ask yourself why and how. Why are you deciding to accomplish this project? What is your motivation behind this objective? Knowing the motivation provides you with a reason and direction for achieving it. Otherwise, you could be stuck and unable to move forward.

Are they regular?

To achieve a long-term goal with the necessary mental energy it is important to keep a schedule and do every day work towards his goal. Inconsistency in your schedule can significantly affect your performance. Are you convinced that you can shed 15kg in just every month? Being inconsistent leads to an absence of motivation and eventually the decision to quit.

Get rid of negative thoughts

How can you achieve your goals if you're affected by negative thoughts of every kind? Negative thoughts cause more paralysis than they create. This is why you need to be able to transform the negative thought into positive real thoughts.

Chapter 13: getting And exoneration

Of Your Mistakes

Making mistakes isn't a good feeling regardless of the situation. When you make a mistake in a heated debate or fail to meet the deadline for work, it's easy to think of yourself as someone who isn't good enough or that you're not enough. Yet, no matter the efforts people make in their lives, there's no one person who is flawless. Humans have complicated minds and emotional states. Once you've learned to manage your emotions, there will be occasions that you do not. The mistake isn't the only thing which is the most important thing However. It's what you do following the error. This chapter will help you on what to do in the aftermath of a mistake to help you respond in a manner that shows your self-love and improves your future.

Realizing That Mistakes Are Normal

Reminisce about a time where a role model made an error. It could be an adult or a family member or a celebrity who was implicated in a scandal. When the people we admire commit mistakes, they are usually blown to the extreme. It is often frustrating, shocking and sometimes even demoralizing to discover that someone you admire so deeply makes an error. But what these shocking events show is the fact that even those we admire can have mistakes.

Being able to accept that failures are part of life is essential to building confidence as well as self-esteem. If someone isn't willing to admit their errors will be feeling guilty when they make a mistake. Although there's nothing wrong with having feelings of sadness, especially in the case of a major mistake, focusing on it can do more harm than positive. Consider what you've discovered about positive thinking so far. When you are thinking negative about yourself, you're not hurting anyone else but yourself.

Gaining Perspective on Mistakes

If someone makes a mistake One of the most important concerns they face is "Why?" They may be curious about what makes them different or why they keep making mistakes. The mistakes that happen can be due to a variety of reasons. Here's several of them.

* You're on auto-pilot. Humans are creatures of habit. The brain is always on the move trying to keep everything going smoothly in your body. To lessen stress and the number of things the brain has to concentrate on, it switches into auto-pilot mode. This is the point where consciousness is shut off and you do the things you normally do without much effort. This is the reason why the drive to work every morning appears effortless and natural. This is also it is the reason why you choose an unintentional exit on the

highway to take the child for soccer training when your brain is directing your work. Although these routines can be beneficial, they may result in mistakes. If you're continually making mistakes in autopilot, practice mindfulness exercises to help stay focused on the present moment.

* You're experiencing intense emotions. People are more likely to act out in a bizarre manner when they're upset. If you're feeling depressed and hungry it is more likely to indulge when you are hungry. If you're angry with people, you're more likely to fight with them or even say rude things. This is normal when you're experiencing an extreme emotional surge. You can manage your emotions more effectively by using some of the techniques we'll be discussing in the future. But, remember that there could be extremely emotional situations in which you'll have a difficult time putting your knowledge to good use.

* You lack experience. People are particularly susceptible to making mistakes when doing something completely new. This is not something should be taken as a cause for discouragement. In the end, there's no one in the world who is a master at all things. If you make a mistake, remember that you've been taught the wrong way to go about it. This is just one step further from gaining the knowledge you require to complete the job precisely. It takes about ten years to be an expert in certain areas. If you're worried that you're not ahead of the latest trends, conduct some research and then use it to establish goals for yourself.

* You're not taking proper care of yourself. People are more likely to commit mistakes or act out in a way that is unnatural when they're tired hungry, stressed, or overly full. It is crucial to take your time sleeping every night, and work hard to eat healthy food and make time to unwind. If you don't take good care of yourself, you are

more likely to make mistakes. This means that you will spend more time working on the issue, and not spending enough time looking after yourself.

Be aware of the difference between mistakes and poor Decisions

It is impossible to excuse every unfavorable outcome you experience in your life because of an error. It's not a sin to stay up late and watch your favorite TV show instead of taking a break due to an exam tomorrow. It's an error. Going on a scenic route to an appointment in the midst of being in a hurry is a mistake but it isn't a mistake to make.

A key difference between errors and poor decisions is the way you deal with the consequences. Both need to be addressed when you want to keep moving towards your goals and be the most successful person you can be. If you do make poor decisions take note of what you're doing. Poor decisions are a type of self-sabotage.

In this case, you deliberately decide to create obstacles in your life. It is possible that the attraction of self-sabotage diminishes when you boost your self-esteem and live your most fulfilling life.

The Positive Side of Mistakes

Every mistake can be an chance to improve. Anyone making bacon the very first time may raise the temperature to high heat as they would like the bacon to be crisp. If they do this, however, at an even higher temperature the bacon sticks to the pan and grease begins flying around. The bacon is not crisp, it burns. This is a minor error however it is one that shows that bacon is best cooked at a moderate heat instead of raising it to a high temperature. When the next time someone decides to cook bacon, they'll alter the temperature in accordance with the recipe. They know this since they did the wrong thing at the beginning.

Every mistake is a learning experience. It shouldn't be considered an issue but as an opportunity to reconsider. If someone makes a remark that is hurtful when they're angry in an argument may regret it in the future. The regret can be better spent looking back at the mistakes they made. It is possible to think about the intense emotions that triggered anger as well as the triggers that led them to be so upset. If they experienced an anger outburst due to keeping something in a bottle for a long time it could be necessary reconsider how they deal with issues or how they express their feelings.

The main benefit of being able to accept and grow from your mistakes is that you develop the confidence to experiment with new things. Perfectionists do not attempt something until they are confident that they can succeed. But, this can hold them from taking on tasks they're not sure about. They aren't able to try new ideas or complete projects due to the fact that they lack the confidence to carry out their plans.

Why Forgiving Your Own Mistakes is Important

Imagine for the moment that you're on a staircase. This staircase symbolizes the path towards a destination. As you walk up the stairs, about the middle, you make an accident. What should you do? Are you going to get up and continue to move ahead? Or, would you take a tumble down the stairs and ruin every progress you've achieved in achieving your target?

If you are not able to accept the mistakes you made and self-defeating, you're sabotaging yourself. Making mistakes can trigger feelings of frustration, sadness anger, guilt, and sadness. All of these feelings are negative and uncomfortable. Although experiencing them after an error is normal but lingering on them is a way to punish yourself. If you make mistakes and are unable to let it go and then you cause yourself suffering and negative feelings in order to try to harm your self-esteem.

Be aware that you are human. Be prepared not to avoid mistakes. There isn't one living individual who has never made a mistake during their life. There are mistakes made by people since they're young, and all they do is learn from their mistakes. Consider the number of cups toddlers have to spill before they are able to drink from the cup. They're all mistakes, but even if they didn't make those mistakes, the child would never have had the chance to drink from a cup.

Strategies for Forgiving Yourself

It is much easier to say than it is to do. Although it becomes more comfortable to accept forgiveness for yourself (and others) as you get more comfortable however, it can be a challenge initially. These strategies can make letting the past go more easy:

• Separate yourself from past experiences. Each person's history is unique with some being more dark than others. If you're struggling with a mistake in your history, the most effective option to let yourself forgive yourself is to be focused on the change. If you're feeling so unhappy by your behavior that it's affecting you today, consider separating yourself from the previous mistakes. Be aware that at any time you can use your power to alter how you conduct yourself and be an improved person. This is not possible when you're constantly contemplating who you were once. Instead, strive to become an improved version of yourself.

You should be able to recognize your strengths. A boost in confidence after making an error helps you appreciate your strengths and counterbalance your weak points. This is especially helpful where you've excelled in something, but made an error in the same subject. For example, whereas one may fail in cooking bacon in the first attempt however, they may have a very good taste and be adept at mixing spices. They're not bad in the kitchen, but they require a bit more practice in certain areas.

• Make mistakes in the process of learning. It is crucial to forgive yourself as it could be harmful to trust your judgement too excessively. Research has shown that people who have a high degree of expertise in their area (like physicians) tend to be less likely spot and rectify mistakes since they are convinced that their judgment is reliable. If you're open to errors, it provides you with the chance of identifying and fixing mistakes before they become an issue. Furthermore being willing to errors, you're offering yourself the opportunity to test your self-confidence, without worrying about the consequences.

Conclusion

If you've completed the last chapter of this guide I hope you know how you can begin to improve your self-esteem as well in a plan or three or two that you're eager to test for the first time. Before you decide to begin to give everything you have but, it's crucial to set realistic expectations about what level of success you can expect within the next few months.

Although it's possible that some individuals experience huge success right from the beginning, it's an unfortunate reality of life that they're the exception rather than the norm. This means that you will experience some sort of learning curve especially when you're just beginning to figure out what you can do to succeed. It's normal, but If you are patient, you will be more confident and successful because of it. Instead of putting your hopes overly optimistic consider the time you spend building your self-esteem as a race, not a sprint so that being slow and steady wins every time.

Are you able to apply the knowledge that you've learned to help keep your self-esteem high? Take a look at the confidence you have in your loved family members. Do you know what kind of confidence they have in themselves? How can they maintain their confidence in themselves? If they lack confidence can it impact you and also the extent to which you are able to be a part of their circle? What can you say to people who are not confident?

While the focus of this course is building self-esteem by positive thinking and positive activities and a more positive mental state can make you open to a myriad of physical and mental changes. While changing your mindset as well, you can also change your behavior and capabilities by acquiring new skills.

The main concern is that you possess an enormous influence on your happiness and can greatly increase it by taking a step and changing the frame of mind about you. You are the one who decides for your life. Your happiness is contingent in an amazing part of how you reveal about what you do to yourself and how you perceive the reality of your life.

The development of self-esteem is essential. When we discover how to love ourselves, we strive for a better life and a happier relationship, a better job or recovery from slavery. Changes to the deep, established beliefs we hold about ourselves isn't an easy task. Many times, doctors recommend a particular therapy (typically cognitive Behavioral Therapy) in order to discover the core reasons behind our negative self-talk.

The main goal is to change these negative beliefs into positive ones. Finding out how to value and view your body and brain with a dependable method of living is crucial. An exercise routine, a healthy diet and meditation could be the very first steps towards restoring your physical and emotional certainty. The ability to be completely captivating with the people whom we cherish is significant. Feeling loved and supported (and being able to show love and support in return) is a fantastic method to increase confidence. In the event that you don't have immediate family or friends At that point, take into consideration joining a support group or volunteering. Giving back to others is an incredible way to help yourself.

www.ingramcontent.com/pod-product-compliance
Lightning Source LLC
Chambersburg PA
CBHW060333030426
42336CB00011B/1329